The First HMS Invincible
(1747–58)

Her Excavations (1980–1991)

by

John M. Bingeman

Government Licensee

Oxbow Books

Oxford and Oakville

Published by
Oxbow Books, Oxford, UK

ISBN 978-1-84217-393-0

A CIP record for this book is available from the British Library

This book is available direct from
Oxbow Books, Oxford, UK
(Phone: 01865-241249; Fax: 01865-794449)

and

The David Brown Book Company
PO Box 511, Oakville, CT 06779, USA
(Phone: 860-945-9329; Fax: 860-945-9468)

or from our website
www.oxbowbooks.com

Front cover: Invincible *stranded on Sunday 19th February 1758. Oil painting by John R. Terry.*
Photograph Maurice Pavey
Back cover, left to right: the 14-second sandglass, photograph John Bingeman.
21 in. single block, photograph Geoff Lee.
Chris Underwood recording the hull structure, photograph Chris Dobbs.
Pewter spoon bowl with a 'capstan' engraving, photograph John Ambler.

Printed in Great Britain by
Short Run Press, Exeter

Contents

Note: All scales used are indicative; actual measurements are given when known.
The term 'HMS' has been used for the title of the Book to clarify her warship status; this abbreviation was not generally used until about 1820.

Foreword

by Doctor Margaret Rule, CBE, FSA

In the nineteenth and early twentieth centuries archaeological survey of ancient sites by amateurs was the norm. Scholars, including men of medicine and the church undertook survey and excavation as a commitment quite separate from their day to day responsibilities. The journals of the county archaeology societies are littered with their reports and these reports provide the foundations of modern archaeology. This tradition of amateur dedication and commitment continues today but this publication may well be the last to record work on an important ship by a team of amateur, that is unpaid, archaeologists.

In July 1980 a public notice posted by the Department of Trade recorded its intention to protect a site within a 100m radius around an unidentified wreck lying in the sea bed off the south coast of England. This proposal was based on evidence submitted by Commander John Bingeman, a serving naval officer and an experienced amateur archaeologist. In the following September this site became the twenty-second historic wreck to be protected under the authority of the Protection of Wrecks Act of 1973. John was granted a licence to continue to survey and excavate the ship later identified as *Invincible*, a 74 gun warship that foundered in 1758. I agreed to serve as his Archaeological Director and this publication is the result of 29 years work by John and his team of volunteers.

After lengthy discussions we agreed to carry out a limited series of excavations to identify the wreck and define her importance. The areas of intrusion were limited to hand excavation using small airlifts to take away detritus and care was taken to limit any intrusion in the seabed to an area that could be back filled and stabilized each autumn. When John accepted the licence he was aware of the challenges he faced, but as the investigation developed his commitment to the work and his sense of privilege grew. His team of totally committed and dedicated amateurs all recognized that being an underwater archaeologist is not a nine to five job.

In 1974 I was invited to become a member of the Advisory Committee formed to review all applications to the Department of Trade for designation of a site as a protected wreck and approve licences to work on designated sites. I remained a member of that committee for nearly twenty years.

With other members of the committee I had pressed for years for legislation to protect our underwater cultural heritage. Unfortunately, under this new legislation, there was no budget to fund a diving inspectorate and nothing had been done to remove historic wrecks from the constraints and potentially seductive inducements of the Merchant Shipping Act 1871. A small band of professional archaeologists, orchestrated by the late Joan du Plat Taylor, ran extensive training courses in the philosophy and practice of underwater survey and excavation for amateur divers.

Other members of the Advisory Committee on Historic Wreck Sites were eminent scholars; historians, archaeologists, lawyers and museum directors, but only two of us were divers! Our opportunity to visit sites was limited. In the late 1970s, when the Secretary of State for Trade and Industry visited the *Mary Rose* site we were delighted that his Parliamentary Private Secretary, John Prescott MP, was able to dive with me and later brief his minister with an eyewitness account of what he had seen.

By 1987 the newly formed Archaeology Diving Unit (ADU), based at St Andrew's University was contracted to visit sites and report back to the Advisory Committee. They brought with them good equipment and at last the potential to advise the licensee on site. Since that time divers from the ADU and its successor, the diving unit from Wessex Archaeology, have visited the site from time to time and a multibeam acoustic survey carried out by Wessex Archaeology verified the manual survey completed by John and his team.

The responsibility for safety dominated the work programme: safety for the divers, a mixed team of amateur, professional and naval divers; and safe, non-destructive excavation of the ship and her contents. Under current Health and Safety Executive regulations, it is difficult for amateur and professional archaeologists to dive together. The satisfaction achieved when amateurs and professionals consult after working together underwater is missing under the present regulations.

Every object had to be recorded underwater and stabilized, photographed, drawn and conserved as soon as possible. A conservation laboratory was established and a professional conservator was engaged to deal with the growing collection of objects and prepare them for public display. Since 1980 it is estimated that over three million people have seen objects from *Invincible* displayed at Chatham Historic Dockyard and the Royal Naval Base in Portsmouth. These exhibitions open a door to the past and the enthusiasm engendered in young visitors spills over into a caring interest in their cultural heritage.

The ship remains in the seabed covered with a veil of mud and sand and John still holds a licence to monitor the site (at his own expense) and report any exposure of the vulnerable timbers. Preservation *in situ* is a hopeless dream; beam trawls plough the upper levels of sand bars and ships occasionally drag their anchors. In November 1996, the merchantman MV AMER VED had engine failure and went aground within the *Invincible* protected area. Her anchor became entangled with the timbers of the wreck and the wreck buoy. When the ship was recovered at high tide, she took away the wreck buoy and sinker. Substantial damage occurred and this would not have been prevented by covering with sand bags or with terram, an inert blanket used to protect the *Mary Rose* timbers when they lay exposed within the seabed in 1980.

In 1974 when I joined the Advisory Committee on Historic Wreck Sites the Chairman, the late Viscount Runciman of Doxford, shared with us his opinion that the best custodian for an underwater monument would be a dedicated licensee. I am sure that he was right.

Margaret Rule
Chichester 2009

Acknowledgements

Over the last twenty-nine years so many people have helped in some way or another that I apologise in advance to those I don't mention.

Until I retired from the Royal Navy, members of the Portsmouth Royal Naval Sub-Aqua Club were my workforce both at the Needles Historic Wreck site and, in the early days, at this site. Since sailors came and went on deployment, three Ministry of Defence civilian members provided the Club's continuity. They are: Norman Bradburn, or 'Brad' to his friends, who could fix anything from radars to boats' engines; Peter Hales a professional diver who was responsible for many of the excellent artefact photographs; and John Terry whose drawings and paintings have enhanced this publication.

The former *Mary Rose* Trust divers helped from time to time. In particular thanks are due to: Dr Alex Hildred, Barrie Andrian, and Ian Oxley for undertaking the second pre-disturbance survey; Dr Jonathan Adams for his outstanding underwater sketches; and to Christopher Dobbs for his underwater photography.

Following the Project's 1987 re-financing until excavations concluded in 1990, diving was carried out by a core team of four made up from: Chris Underwood, David Burden, Adrian Barak, Steve Waring, Liz Cornwell, and the always present Licensee. We were assisted on occasions by Peter Ewens, Charles Pochin, Damien Sanders and Bob Stewart.

Arthur Mack with John Broomhead started the whole Project. They both continue to be involved to this present day. Solicitor John Saulet put the Project on a financial footing – without it, the excavations would never have been completed. Simon Aked, a qualified Conservation Officer ran our Conservation Laboratory. Dr David Houghton took a keen interest in our activities, and made up the sixth member of the team. The six of us were individual guarantors of the Project's bank overdraft.

John Broomhead has made a major contribution to this publication by setting the artefact record on an Access data base which can be interrogated by individual item or by group description. His data base has been further enhanced by including illustrations, work undertaken by Brandon Mason who has been employed by the *Hampshire and Wight Trust for Maritime Archaeology* to digitise the *Invincible* archive held by the Licensee. The digitising of the archive was made possible by a Heritage Lottery Grant. The artefact data base can be found in the rear pocket on the CD-ROM.

Fisherman Arthur Mack has been a close friend ever since he walked into my office in March 1980. He has been my boatman, diver's attendant, research assistant, and has a phenomenal memory. His contribution to the Project and this publication has been continuous.

Recently, Geoff Lee, Conservation Officer at Chatham Historic Dockyard Trust has been most helpful and provided a number of photographs from the *Invincible Representative Collection* held by the Trust. My thanks are due to the late Mr David White formerly of the National Maritime Museum who is the author of 'Appendix A' which lists all *Invincible*'s dockyard repairs and their costs.

John P. Bethell, neighbour and fellow member of The Society for Nautical Research, has helped me focus on my writing-up of information which can be difficult to express, and corrected my grammatical errors. He has been responsible for enhancing most of the illustrations with his skill using 'Photoshop' software.

Thirty-three years ago, I telephoned Dr Margaret Rule to ask if she would give a lecture to my Sub-Aqua Club, and also if she needed another diver on the *Mary Rose* site. She agreed to both. Two years later she recommended me to the Advisory Committee on Historic Wreck Sites as the person to take over responsibility for the Needles Historic Wreck site – a task I carried out for the next nine years. In the summer of 1980, I needed an Archaeological Director for my application to be the Licensee of this unknown wreck in the Eastern Solent. Despite having a more than full time task with the *Mary Rose* she agreed. Since 1991 when excavations stopped, she has remained my Archaeological Advisor. Over the last year as this publication has been developing, Margaret has studied my drafts; her comments and advice have been invaluable.

My wife Jane has supported and encouraged my underwater activities, put up with artefacts and diving gear around the house, and has knocked my English prose into a more readable fashion.

Finally, I would like to record my thanks to the Society for Nautical Research for a recent contribution towards the cost.

John M. Bingeman
July 2009

Glossary

ACHWS	Advisory Committee on Historic Wreck Sites.
ADM	Admiralty documents in the National Archive.
BM	British Museum.
Coak	Central bronze bearing in a rigging block sheave.
Crank	Oxford Dictionary: 'weak, shaky, liable to capsize'.
Draughts	Detailed ships' plans. At the National Maritime Museum all the ships' plans are kept in the 'Draught Room'.
EDTA	Used in conservation (Ethylenediamine tetra-acetic acid).
Establishment	'Establishment for Men and Guns' for each 'Rate' of ship came into force in 1677 and was extended to standardise ships' dimensions in 1706. As years went by, these specifications tended to inhibit improvement in ship design.
HMA	Hampshire Museum Authority.
HR	Hydrogen reduction furnace used in conservation.
IJNA	International Journal of Nautical Archaeology.
MRT	Mary Rose Trust.
NA	National Archive, Kew, London.
NAS	Nautical Archaeology Society (for training).
Quoin	Wedge to adjust a cannon barrel's elevation.
PCM	Portsmouth City Museums.
PEG	Polyethylene glycol used in conservation.
Rate	First Rates, Second Rates, etc were used to categorise warships depending on the number of guns they carried. Over the years as ships became larger, First Rates became Second Rates, etc.
Truck	Gun carriage wheel. It is also used to describe various pieces of rigging such as: 'shroud truck' and 'parrel truck'.
Treen	Small antique domestic wooden objects.
Vaillant	18th century spelling of 'Valiant', from the French.
WO	War Office documents in the National Archive.

Introduction

The Protection of Wrecks Act 1973 was passed by the United Kingdom's Parliament to preserve the country's underwater heritage. Today in 2009, the Act protects over sixty sites. In 1980 I applied for a Government protection order following the discovery of a wreck by local fisherman Arthur Mack. A licence was granted by the Under-Secretary of State for the Department of Trade following the recommendation of the Advisory Committee for Historic Wreck Sites (ACHWS). This was the twenty-second licence to be granted under the 1973 Act. I subsequently identified the wreck as the Royal Navy's first *Invincible* (1747–58).

Archaeological recoveries have proved that man inhabited 'The Solent' foreshores before 8000 BC, the Palaeolithic period. Underwater searches off the Isle of Wight, opposite Bouldnor Cliff and ten metres below present day sea level, found traces of habitation along the now drowned Solent River with a carbon date of 6000 BC, the Mesolithic period. Chichester, Portchester and Clausentum (Southampton) were all towns established during the Roman occupation (43–410 AD) and were

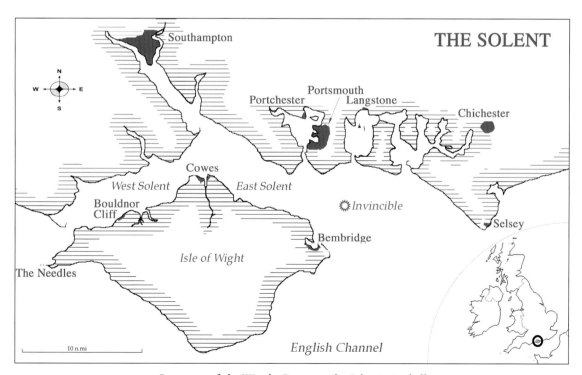

Location of the Wreck. Drawing by John P. Bethell.

served by natural harbours. In Tudor times, Portsmouth had become a Naval Base and has remained the Royal Navy's premier Dockyard to this day as well as an important NATO harbour. It is therefore not surprising that 'The Solent' holds within its waters many wreck sites. Three important historic sites are: the *Grace Dieu* (1418) built by order of King Henry V and destroyed by lightning in 1439; the *Mary Rose* (1509) which capsized while attacking the French in 1545, and will be on display at the Portsmouth Naval Base; and my wreck, the Royal Navy's first *Invincible*, the subject of this publication. With this background, those fortunate to be either professional or amateur archaeologists diving in these murky Solent waters are re-discovering our Nation's history. Among these pages, the reader will find details of artefacts long forgotten.

Invincible was a 74-gun warship that came to grief on Sunday the 19th February 1758 off Portsmouth. She was sailing as part of the expedition to besiege the French Fortress of Louisbourg, Nova Scotia. This was the beginning of a progressive series of military operations leading to the eventual colonisation of Canada.

This publication is the Licensee's record of 29 years' commitment to holding the Government licence for the excavation of the wreck site and for research evaluating the historical importance of the ship and the wreck. Included are: a description of *Invincible's* building as a French warship launched in 1744, her capture in 1747 by the Royal Navy, her foundering in the Solent, and the 1979–1990 excavations of the wreck site. Particular attention is paid to artefacts recovered forming a unique time capsule of an English ship-of-the-line of the mid-18th century. The research following the unexpected recovery of Army uniform buttons is of considerable historical interest.

After the initial tasks of conducting a pre-disturbance survey and successfully convincing the United Kingdom Advisory Committee on Historic Wreck Sites of the need to award a Government protection order, it has been a mammoth undertaking running the Project and keeping abreast of further stringent regulations that came into force during the excavations. My thanks are due to a hundred or so helpers who have given their support without financial reward during the eleven years of excavations. While the costs of the underwater excavations were comparatively small, that of our private conservation laboratory tasked with the conservation and recording of many thousands of artefacts was considerable. The trials and tribulations of conducting the Project and raising the necessary funds are all covered. Apart from the historical importance of excavating *Invincible*, our experience may help future teams undertaking similar projects, especially those concerning the 18th century.

The site is historically important for two reasons: firstly the ship herself, and secondly the contents within her hull.

The Ship, brought into British service when only three years old, was the first newly designed 74-gun warship to be captured from the French. It represented a significant step forward in ship construction and was to become the prototype for a new generation of British men-of-war. After repair, she was commissioned as a flagship which indicates what a fine ship the French had built.

In 1758 when *Invincible* foundered, she was a British ship-of-the-line fully equipped for an expedition abroad. Although her guns and much of her equipment were salvaged at the time, she was subsequently abandoned with a considerable amount of equipment still onboard. The 20th century salvaging of the site's artefacts has provided naval archaeologists and historians with a time capsule of equipment aboard a warship in the mid-18th century. Her loss happened during the Seven Years' War, and less than forty years before the French Revolutionary and Napoleonic Wars, when British warships were frequently engaged with similar equipment onboard.

A number of artefacts have been used as patterns for the manufacture of replicas to restore Admiral

Lord Nelson's flagship, HMS *Victory*, to how she would have been at the time of the Battle of Trafalgar in 1805. *Invincible*'s artefacts also create a historical link between *Victory* and the *Mary Rose*, whose recovery provides a time capsule of the earlier mid-16th century.

In addition, because *Invincible* was carrying troops to Canada, the wreck site contained regimental equipment, including army buttons that pre-dated previously accepted dates and are of significance to army historians.

Details of *Invincible*'s artefacts and their significance will be addressed in the following chapters, and army buttons in Appendix B.

L'Invincible's Captain, Chevalier de St Georges surrenders his sword to Admiral Lord Anson on 14th May 1747 onboard the Prince George following the capture of L'Invincible *at the First Battle of Finisterre.*

1. Historical Importance. Her Loss and Discovery. Working an Historic Wreck Site

Historical Importance

L'Invincible was one of the first three '74-gun ships' conceived by the French, a type of warship chosen by other navies in subsequent years. After her capture and following her arrival at Portsmouth, the Admiralty ordered her to be surveyed[1] in great detail since no similar ship of two and a half decks existed. Four months later, their Lordships were suitably impressed with her qualities, and ordered her to be commissioned as a flagship.[2] She therefore provides a key witness in the controversy concerning the merits of British and French shipbuilding in the 18th century.

The Licensee after identifying the wreck as *Invincible* in September 1980, decided to look further into the subject and her history.

In the 1740s the French, as an emerging colonial power, conceived the idea of building a new design of 74-gun ships for their Navy. The first, the *Terrible* was built at Brest by Francis Coulon, and a further two were laid down at Rochefort. The second of the two designed by Morineau, was called *L'Invincible*, and launched on the 21st October 1744. Her service with the French Navy was short. After a successful deployment to the West Indies, she fought off single-handedly a superior British Force consisting of

Figure 1. Rochefort river bank where Invincible *was built 1742–44. The white building is the dry dock where the* L'Hermione *(1778) replica is being built. Photograph John Bingeman, 2002.*

the *Plymouth* (60), *Strafford* (50) and *Lyme* (24).[3] No mean feat against the English who broke off the engagement first, and on this occasion were convincingly out-gunned by *L'Invincible*. She returned safely to France with her convoy of eighty-one ships.

The Licensee and his wife found forty-eight letters from Versailles in the Rochefort Bibliotheque de la Marie (Archive Office) written during her building between 1741 and 1744. Having navigated the 17 miles of shallow meandering La Charente River in a motor yacht, we could appreciate the real difficulty of moving a large ship with no engine power down to the open sea. This was only possible when spring tides coincided with calm weather. While the correspondence was only one way, it was quite clear that the local difficulties were not always appreciated at Versailles, particularly when *L'Invincible* had to return for further work. On one occasion it took a month to return her down the river. Rochefort's strategic position meant that ships could be built and refitted without the threat of an English attack.

Her Capture

A year later, she was off again in support of an East India convoy. Unfortunately for the French, she was captured near Cape Finisterre after fighting a superior Force of fourteen Ships-of-the-Line under

Figure 2. The Port of Rochefort in 1762 on La Charente River. Invincible *was built in the centre of this picture next to the trees. The Ropery is the long building on the right.*

Figure 3. A French 18th Century model of L'Invincible *in the Rochefort 'Ropery Museum' (Musée d'Art et d'Histoire de Rochefort). Photograph Jane Clarke.*

Admiral Lord Anson. While being towed back to Portsmouth, Anson sent his carpenter onboard to measure her, after commenting that she was 'a prodigious fine ship, and vastly large, I think she is longer than any ship in our Fleet and is quite new.'[4] Back at home, and presumably on the instigation of Anson, the Admiralty tried to circumvent the 1745 Establishment, which had 'no mention of a ship of two and a half decks to carry 74 Guns', and ordered two ships to her design. Both were cancelled for lack of funds when the war ended a few months later.

Admiral of the Fleet Lord Anson (1697–1762)

While a Post-Captain, Admiral of the Fleet Lord George Anson made his name by circumnavigating the World in the *Centurian* between 1740 and 1744. He captured the Spanish treasure ship *Nuestra Señora de Covadonga* off the Phillipines which made him wealthy for life. On return, the treasure was paraded in London in no less than thirty-two wagons! He was promoted Admiral in 1745 and after capturing *Invincible* and other ships was made a Lord in 1748.

To quote the Navy League Journal:[5]

> 'Owing to the sound judgement and practical knowledge displayed by Anson in all naval matters, he exercised great influence at the Admiralty from the time of his appointment. Both the Duke of Bedford and the Earl of Sandwich, the two First Lords under whom he served from 1744 to 1751, placed implicit confidence in him, and allowed themselves to be guided by him in all matters relating to the administrative control of the Navy.'

Figure 4. Admiral Lord Anson by the Portrait Painter, Arthur Pond (1701–1758) (A less well-known early painting of the Admiral, reproduced by kind permission of the National Trust, Shugborough).

In 1745, in response to many complaints that our ships were not as seaworthy as those of the same size built by France and Spain, Anson was responsible for ordering a reassessment for each class of ship. As a result, new draughts (ships' drawings) were carefully worked out for approval by the Admiralty.

Anson had learnt a great deal about ships from his four year circumnavigation. Reading the letters to Anson from both Benjamin Slade (Master Shipwright at Plymouth) and John Goodwin (Master Shipwright at Deptford),[6] helped me to understand that Anson was receiving specialist information enabling him to be the driving force correcting deficiencies in warship design. His personal interest together with advice from Slade and Goodwin ultimately improved ship construction. Admiral Knowles's letter dated 6th Jan. 1744/5[7] shows that Anson was well aware of the hydrodynamics around a ship's hull.

In 1751 he became First Lord of the Admiralty, a post he held apart from a short gap, until his death in 1762. During this time he is credited with affecting much needed reforms in administration and introducing an established system of rating men-of-war. It was his appreciation of *Invincible's* superior build and sailing qualities that were eventually incorporated into ship designs of the Royal Navy. One of his final acts in 1761 was to order the 5th rate 32 gun *Alarm* to be copper sheathed. This successful trial led to the decision to sheathe all ships in 1780.

Anson has been given little credit by Naval Historians for his outstanding contribution to the 18th century Navy.

Figure 5. Engraving of Invincible *(far right) under repair at Portsmouth Dockyard following her capture from the French in 1747.*

Figure 6. Invincible *back in Service with her sails 'backed'. Published by R. Short according to an Act of Parliament April 2nd 1751.*

Invincible (1747–1758)

Armament

Main Deck:	twenty-eight 32-pounders.
Upper deck:	thirty 18-pounders. In 1756 replaced by thirty 24-pounders of the new light weight design.
Quarterdeck:	sixteen 9-pounders
	Total 74 guns

Particulars

Tonnage: 1826
Length of gundeck: 171ft 3in (52.2m)

Figures 7 and 8. Taken from John Fincham's A History of Naval Architecture, *1851.*

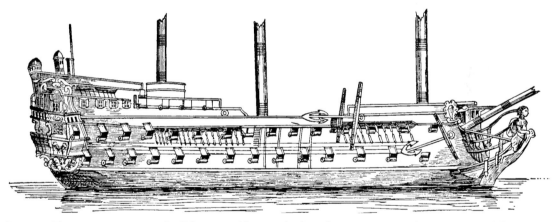

Figure 9. The picture caption reads: "The Invincible *French Ship of war mounting 74 Guns, Captured from France, May 3rd 1747, by Vice Admiral Anson & Rear Admiral Warren." Left hand corner: 'John Charnock Del't' and right hand corner 'Newton Sculp't'. Published as the Act directs March 3rd 1802 by John Sewell, Cornhill, London.*

Length on keel for tonnage: 143ft 6in (43.7m)
Breadth (extreme): 48ft 11in (14.9m)
Depth in hold: 21ft 3in (6.5m)

Invincible retained her original French figurehead of 'Ceres' the Goddess of corn and harvests. In her arms, the Goddess cradles a small sheaf of corn. While not clear in the small engavings, this can be seen in the full sized version of Short's 1751 *Invincible* engraving.

Captain Bentley's Sailing Report for *Invincible*

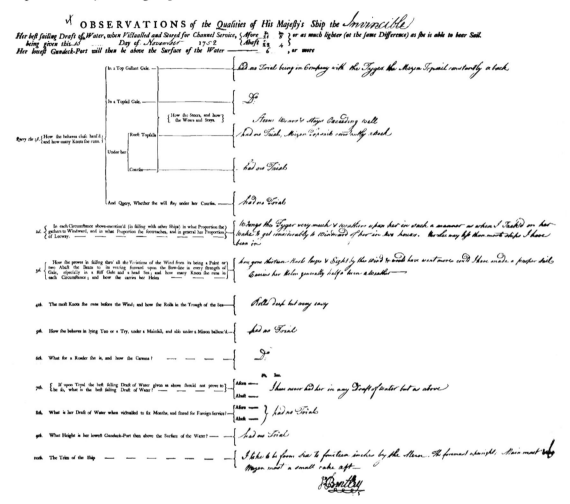

Figure 10. Captain Bentley's sailing report on 15th November 1752 when he recorded a speed of 13 knots. The Report records that the lowest gundeck ports were 6 feet above the waterline.

Rudder Angle Indicator

Invincible's method of steering with a rudder angle indicator prompted the Admiralty to issue a directive on 22nd January 1747/8:

> '*Invincible* a model showing in what manner she is fitted in regard to steering her, to send one to each yard and to cause all His Majesty's Ships to be fitted in that manner for the future.'[10]

The steering indicator showed both the quartermaster and the officer of the watch the angle of the rudder at any given moment. The device in the *Invincible* was apparently built using a graduated scale placed above the wheel on the foremost beam of the poop. This was fitted with a pointer which presumably was linked to the wheel by ropes.[11]

Problem how to 'Rate' *Invincible*

No similar class of ship had existed previously. After her capture, the authorities had found it difficult to 'rate' her, since she was larger than the second rates but only carried 74-guns. Her shortfall in guns was compensated by her 36-pounders (French guns subsequently replaced with British 32-pounders) being six feet above the waterline;[12] the British first and second rates' guns were only three to four feet above the waterline, preventing the use of their heaviest guns in all but the calmest of seas. Admirals, particularly Anson, were convinced that '74s' were the future of warship design. This means that the capture of *Invincible* revolutionised British warship design; they became the backbone of the Fleet for over half a century. In 1778, only 20 years after her demise, there were fifty-eight '74s' in His Majesty's Royal Navy.[13] At Trafalgar, sixteen of the thirty-three ships were 74-gun ships.

Comparison of French and British Ships after 1707

At first glance the French and British draughts seem similar; on close examination, it is evident that the French designs have a fuller bow and slimmer stern; in other words a better shaped hull for speed. According to Captain Bentley's sailing report dated 13th November 1752,[14] *Invincible* was capable of 13 knots, while contemporary British ships recorded speeds of no more than 11 knots. Benjamin Slade, the Surveyor at Plymouth and kinsman of Sir Thomas Slade, had been aware of the difference when writing to Anson on 21st July 1747 about the recently captured 24 gun French privateer *Tiger (Tygre)*:

> 'I am strongly of opinion the present draughts of the 24 gunships are too full aft, and that the *Tiger* is as much the contrary, ...'[15]

Conventionally, ships are trimmed by the stern. *Invincible* was 15 inches deeper by the stern. Naval Officers were finding that by trimming with the bow down, their ships would sail faster. This endorsed the fact that British ships were too full aft and by sinking the bow gave a better hydrodynamic flow around the hull and therefore more speed. The *Royal George* was previously 14 inches down by the stern and by trimming her 3 inches down by the bow sailed better. ' ... and it was found so in most of the other classes'.[16] The memorandum goes on to compare the *Royal George's* sailing with the 'old *Invincible'*.

Shortcomings with British Ships

In 1747, there had been complaints from sea officers about the poor sailing qualities of the new 24-gun ships designed by the Naval Surveyor, Sir Jacob Ackworth. The Admiralty Board decided to order two new 24-gun ships outside the Establishment. Since Anson and Benjamin Slade had already been discussing their shortcomings, it was no coincidence that it was Slade who was ordered to build a ship, in all respects a copy of the *Tiger (Tygre)*, with the greatest possible expedition. This can perhaps be seen as the precedent that, ten years later, allowed the Navy Board to order two copies of the *Invincible* to be named *Valiant* and *Triumph*.[17]

The building of the *Valiant* took place at Chatham between 1757 and 1759. In 1988 Chatham Historic Dockyard Trust set up a £4M exhibition called 'Wooden Walls' to commemorate this event. The exhibition is housed in the Old Mast House and Mould Loft which dates back to 1753, and records *Valiant's* building through the eyes of John North, her carpenter and William Crockwell, his apprentice. Appropriately, the exhibition is enhanced with displays of *Invincible's* artefacts.

In 1802, her sistership the *Triumph* was described as 'a ship which, for the space of more than twenty years, was considered the finest of her class then existing'[18] – a glowing testimony to Pierre Morineau's French built *Invincible* captured by Admiral Lord Anson in 1747.

To summarise: the capture of *Invincible* with her 'modern' construction techniques, the extensive use of iron knees, spaciousness and superior sailing qualities can claim to have quite literally revolutionised the design of future 74-gun ships in the Royal Navy. By the end of the century there were no less than seventy of these 74-gun ships, the backbone of the Fleet.

Shipbuilding Britain vs France

There are varying opinions on the relative merits of British and French shipbuilding. It is fair to say that both shipbuilding industries had their strengths and both regularly cribbed ideas from each other. British shipbuilding was constrained by various 'Establishments' laying down precise size and the amount of timber to be used for each class of warship to prevent shipbuilders from cheating on Government contracts. However, it also had the adverse effect of stifling design improvements.

The French *Académie Royale des Sciences* from its inception in the late 17th century had been the centre where theories for improving ship design had been developed. By the 1730s academics rather than naval officers or shipbuilders would provide expert advice; however these ideas were not always adopted. Also the recruiting of foreign shipwrights and recalling French carpenters from abroad all contributed to future warship development. In 1741, the term *constructeur* came into being, the role taking an elevated social position within the navy's hierarchy.[19] Formal training was introduced for ship constructors with the setting up of a school in Paris. The courses lasted between six and seven years and included theoretical and practical studies afloat.

> 'Constructors sailed onboard their own ships during campaigns to study the effect of wind and sea on the new methods of building and to examine the security of the mast in ships, perpendicular stern posts and other innovations.'[20]

This coincided with the introduction of the famous French seventy-four gun ships.

In Britain in the 1740s, there was conflict between the Admiralty and the Navy Board over the shortcomings of our warships, and how they could be improved. The creation of the 1745 Establishment by the Navy Board did little to rectify the situation and dissension continued between the two authorities. Because of the differing views, the Establishment was rigorously enforced by the Navy Board and any divergence had to receive Privy Council approval. This had not been the case previously, when a certain amount of licence could be taken by Master Shipwrights.

The problem with British shipbuilding is clearly stated by Charles Derrick, Clerk of the Navy Board in his memoirs when he refers to 'a general complaint of His Majesty's Navy in 1744–1745', that:

> 'their scantlings were not so large and strong as they should be; that they did not carry their guns a proper height above the water (like those of other nations). That they were very crank* and heeled too much in blowing weather; and they did not carry so great of weight of metal as ships of the enemy, whose batteries were said to be always open.'[21]

British lower 3 decker gun ports were three to four feet above the waterline, while the French-built 2 decker *Invincible*'s were six feet. In effect this meant that most of our 3 deckers were in fact 2 deckers in any but the calmest of seas.

*Oxford Dictionary defines 'crank' as: liable to capsize.

As late as 1780, Admiral Kempenfelt wrote to Middleton, Comptroller of the Navy:

'The want of a good foundation laid of mathematical knowledge prevents our builders from rising to eminence; for want of this light, they are often obliged to grope in the dark, they guess, because they have not the mathematics to calculate certainly; when they give their bottom any particular form, they guess at the effect.'[22]

Over the Channel the French constructors, uninhibited by the constraints of the British Establishment, were free to use the developing science of naval architecture and scientific knowledge to improve ship design.

The French influence

The two significant French influences in mid-eighteenth century were: fairer lines to the ship's stern and, changing stern posts from around 12 degrees to near vertical. These changes, and in particular the less 'full' sterns, significantly improved a ship's speed. The illustration compares British hulls prior to the capture of the French *Invincible* in 1747, and subsequent British hulls. Referring back to stern posts, the French constructors – the British only had Master shipwrights – appreciated the effect of angled rudders versus vertical rudders. When turning, the angled rudder acts to pull the stern more deeply into the sea slowing the vessel; this adverse effect does not happen with a near vertical stern post.[23]

British 74s

The British started building their first 74s in the early 1750s and it is worth noting that they were slightly smaller than the French models. They were not entirely successful, and led to the Admiralty Board's decision on the 21st May, 1757 to build the *Triumph* at Woolwich and the *Valiant* at Chatham, using *Invincible* as the model. To quote an extract from the letter of authority:[24]

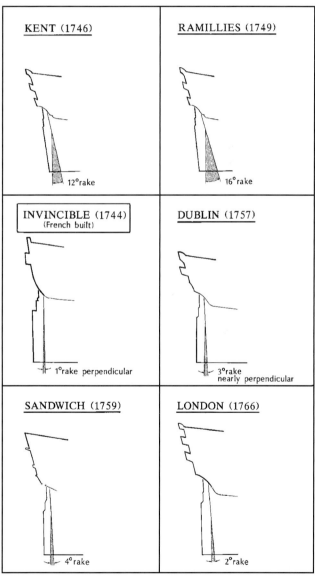

Figure 11. Rudder rake on British warships before and after the capture of Invincible. *Drawing by John R. Terry.*

'....and experience having shown that His Majesty's Ship the Invincible is in every respect, the very best ship of her Class, and answers all purposes that can be desired of a Ship of War. We do therefore hereby desire and direct you to cause the two beforementioned Ships to be Built by the Draught of the Invincible, and in every respect of the same Scantlings, notwithstanding any former Orders to the contrary'

When Captain Rodney was sailing the new British 74-gun ship *Dublin*, ordered on the 26th August 1755, he complained that the rudder was too large and that the poop-deck lifted under the press of canvas.[25] This illustrates the lack of technical understanding in British shipbuilding; clearly the British did not appreciate that by half copying the French they were introducing problems. The traditional British rudder used on a 12 to 16 degree stern post was unnecessarily large when fitted to a near vertical stern post causing additional torque, and twice broke *Dublin's* rudder head.

These lessons were learnt and future ships were greatly improved during the second half of the 18th century.

French influence on Naval Gunnery

To some, it may be near heresy to suggest that French technology influenced British shipbuilding; however, it now seems that not only shipbuilding but also British gun design was influenced by the French!

In December 1755, the Office of Ordnance ordered *Invincible's* thirty 18-pounders to be exchanged for 24-pounders.[26] This order to fit heavier ordnance would at first sight seem foolhardy since it increased top weight and in action would cause extra strain to the ship's side. In fact, neither of these risks were taken.

The London Magazine of June 1747,[27] reported that the French 64-gun ship *Mars* was captured with documents relating to experiments in which lighter guns with smaller charges were used to fire large shot. The French found that with smaller charges 'a bullet, which can just pass through a piece of timber, and loses almost all its motion thereby, has a better chance of rendering and fracturing it, than if it passed through it with a much greater velocity'. The advantages were many; lighter guns were easier to operate and smaller charges not only saved powder but kept the guns cooler and quieter, 'and at the same time more effectually injuring the Vessels of the Enemy'. With Anson's blessing, the theories expressed in the *Mars's* documents were followed up by Mr Benjamin Robins, a member of the Royal Society, who had been working on similar ideas. The next we hear about these new Guns was in *The Gentleman's Magazine* in August 1755:[28] 'Lord Anson and other Lords of the Admiralty have been down to Woolwich to see a proof of some new invented guns that are but half the ordinary weight and will do as much execution.'

It seems likely that the Admiralty would request the Board of Ordnance to order the new light weight 24 pounders for trial in *Invincible*, since she was not subject to the constraining regulations of the Establishment which laid down the size of guns for each Rate of ship. *Invincible's* ordnance stores list refers to 'Quoins for quoining guns of the new pattern'[29] and a further Office of Ordnance letter about *Invincible* refers to giving, '...directions for the New 24 Pounder Carriages...'.[30]

Cannon lock trial

Invincible was also one of thirteen ships selected to try out new cannon locks to speed up the rate of fire.[31] The order gave instructions for the quarterdeck 9-pounders to be fitted with locks. Shortly after she ran aground six of these guns were thrown overboard 'in order to bring her on an even keel'.[32] To the south of the wreck's present position there are magnetometer readings which optimistically might be interpreted as the quarterdeck guns complete with locks. One of *Pomone's* (launched in 1805) 18-pounders on 'The Needles' site, Isle of Wight, still had a lock when recovered 171 years later – see illustrations of *Pomone's* cannon locks in Chapter 5, Figs. 228, 229 and 230.

Invincible's cannon lock trial may explain the finding of over 2,500 flints, in five sizes, thought to be too large for muskets, illustrated in Fig 199.

Disasters – Louisbourg Expeditions 1757 and 1758

In 1757, *Invincible*, commanded by Captain John Bentley, was part of a large expedition under the command of Vice Admiral the Honourable Edward Boscawen to oust the French from the Fortress of Louisbourg in Nova Scotia, Canada. The Fleet had arrived too late in the season and the ships had been severely mauled by appalling September weather. *Invincible*, among those severely damaged, sailed back to Portsmouth under jury rig.

The next year a second expedition was underway with *Invincible* appointed to carry Major-General Jeffery Amherst, the newly appointed Commander-in-Chief, North America. He had not yet arrived back from the Continent and was expected to join when the ship arrived off Plymouth. Also taking passage were 45 soldiers from Cornwallis's Regiment (24th Regiment of Foot) and fifteen unnamed supernumeries. The supernumeries may have been army officers, a hypothesis based on twelve different regimental officers' buttons recovered during excavations – see Appendix B. Further evidence comes from a letter[33] from Barrington, Secretary for War, to Admiral Boscawen informing him that fifteen unattached army officers were to go onboard the Fleet, as reinforcements.

The 18-gun sloop, *Countess of Gramont* (the recently captured French *Comtesse de Grammont*) was sent ahead on the 18th February to New York with instructions to the Lieutenant Governor, General Abercrombie, from the Secretary of State and Secretary at War to prepare for the Louisbourg attack and send troops to Halifax to join up with the Expedition.[34]

At 0230 on Sunday, 19th February 1758 Admiral Boscawen ordered his Squadron at St Helens Roads to weigh anchor; winds were favourable to carry the Expedition down Channel. Disastrously, *Invincible* ran aground and would no longer be part of the Expedition. Boscawen's Squadron now consisted of twelve ships [90-gun *Namur* (Flagship); 84-gun *Royal William*; 80-gun *Princess Amelia*; 66-gun *Lancaster*; 28-gun: *Trent* and *Shannon*; 20-gun *Kennington*; 12-gun *Etna*; and the fireship *Lightning*] plus three transports.[35] He was joined by further ships off Plymouth and Ireland.

The Squadron had increased to a Fleet of 277 ships including 49 warships at the time of the assault on Louisbourg (to be followed by the attack on Quebec). Volunteer James Thompson (Fraser's Highlanders) described the ships in action off Louisbourg:[36]

'Nothing could be like it, and as our ships of war kept up a fire upon the (French) batteries to cover our landings, there was a terrific hullabaloo.'

'Our Fleet, as it seemed to me from the high shore, made a noble appearance, and looked as if the bowsprit of every one was made fast to the stern of the next to it – they stretched across the whole Harbour.'

On the 2nd June, the Louisbourg attack was against tough opposition. Three thousand, five hundred regular French forces, civilians and some Indians manned batteries guarding the strategic landing beaches. Finally driven back from the batteries, the French retreated to the Louisbourg Fortress where they were kept under continuous bombardment until they capitulated on the 26th July 1758.[37] The Garrison numbered 5637 soldiers and sailors at the time of the surrender.

Figure 12. The restored Fortress of Louisbourg in the 1990s. By kind permission of Warren Gordon.

Louisbourg Fortress

Founded in 1713, the Fortress of Louisbourg and supporting batteries were completely destroyed by the Royal Engineers in 1758 to deny any future use by the French. In 1928 the site was declared a National Historic Site, and in 1960 a Canadian Royal Commission decided to start re-constructing the Fortress to its 18th century condition. In 1995, the Licensee and his wife stayed at Louisbourg to visit the Fortress and to see the beaches and French batteries where our troops had fought their way ashore in June 1758.

The loss of Invincible

Meanwhile, back here in the Solent *Invincible*'s problems had started when her anchor stuck on the seabed despite 384 men powering her two double capstans. To increase the pull a large treble purchase was set along the upper deck with a further 100 men. This finally freed the anchor, but more problems arose when the anchor impaled itself on the bow cutwater. While trying unsuccessfully to free the anchor, *Invincible* drifted back towards Portsmouth before tacking northeast in the prevailing east-south-easterly wind. An angle of 60° was the closest that square rigged ships could sail into the wind. When the leadsman called 7¼ fathoms, the Master Henry Adkins ordered the helm to be put over. The tiller jammed when they attempted to go about. The Quartermaster Thomas Moody was sent to investigate and found that the Gunner had already cleared the tiller tackle falls in the Gunroom. But it was all too late; the ship missed stays and grounded on 'The Horse' part of the Dean Sands (Description based on Court Martial transcript).[38]

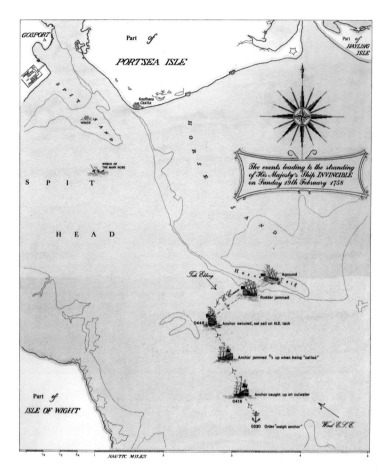

Figure 13. Invincible's *movements on Sunday 19th February leading to her stranding. John R. Terry's illustration is based on using Lieutenant Murdoch Mackenzie's 1783 Chart.*

Assistance

The '*Journal of the Proceedings of his Majesty's Squadron under the Command of the Hon'ble Edward Boscawen, Admiral of the Blue to North America*', written onboard the 90 gun *Namur* while sailing out of the Solent, recorded:[39]

'At daylight saw a ship a ground on the Dean Sand, with a signal of distress out, and several boats about her; which proved to be the Invincible.'

While Boscawen's '*Journal of Proceedings...*' record several boats about *Invincible*, the *Royal George* log records that two boats were sent to assist *Invincible* 'but the wind blowing fresh they put back again'.

The *Royal George* log records the weather over the next three days as:

Monday 20th 'First part hard gales and squally'
Tuesday 21st 'Fresh gales and squally with rain ...'
Wednesday 22nd 'Strong gales and hazey ...' The day *Invincible* fell over on her beam ends.

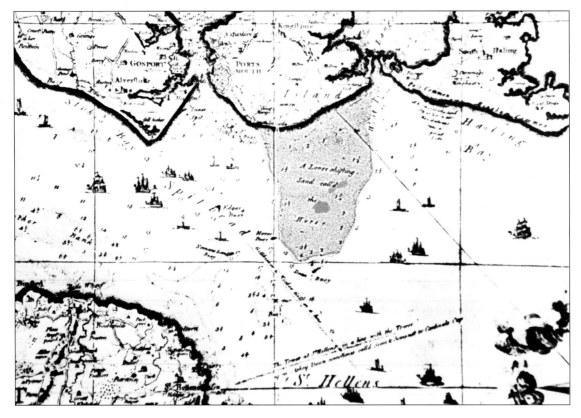

Figure 14. Part of 'Map of Hampshire' showing the Horse Sands. Isaac Taylor 1759.

Commander Robertson, Second-in-Command of the *Royal Sovereign*, records in his journal that his ship was more helpful by assisting with their Longboat and two more boats on both Monday and Tuesday. The final entry in his Journal on the Tuesday reads: 'Sent 6 casks of water to the *Invincible*'.

As one would expect, the majority of the assistance came from the Dockyard. Various hoys (sailing barges) came out to lighten her by taking off guns and other stores. On the Monday at high water, directed by Mr Gastrin, the Dockyard's Master Attendant and the pilot Mr Locket, the ship's company tried to drive *Invincible* off under full sail without success.

Invincible aground

Today on the Horse Tail there is only 18 feet of water at low water and *Invincible* drew 23 feet by the stern. Going aground on a sandbank should not have been too disastrous. An attempt to kedge her off to the south failed. In the Court Martial proceedings when questions were asked whether the anchor had holed the hull, it was denied that she had 'bilged' herself. Whatever the reason, her hold soon became flooded to a depth of 12 feet. *Invincible* had four chain pumps to remove water. It is claimed that one chain pump could remove a ton of water in 45 seconds with four fresh men. Despite all four pumps working continuously, she remained flooded. Whether the anchor had holed the hull or whether the grounding had opened up seams is not known. Extra pumps were brought out from the Dockyard while guns and stores were being landed in hoys (sailing barges). Next, they tried to drive her off under full sail as directed by Mr Gastrin, the Dockyard's Master Attendant and Mr Locket, the Pilot. No success. First one chain pump broke, then another, and another. The weather deteriorated and the seas were breaking over her. Late on the fourth day she fell over on her port side beam ends. Her fate was sealed. For the next three weeks, Bentley personally supervised the removal of stores and rigging. The 24 and 32-pounder guns had been landed during salvage attempts and six of the 9-pounder quarterdeck guns were jettisoned when she first went aground. Further stores were recovered during the summer months including her masts and spars.

Invincible's *hull was suspect*

In September 1757, *Invincible* had been through a hurricane when taking part in the abortive First Louisbourg Expedition. She had been thrown onto her beam ends, lost her mainmast, broken her rudder, and was seriously flooded. Only the weather moderating saved her from being wrecked on the Cape Breton Coast. The 60-gun *Windsor* towed her out to sea, to enable her to make repairs and set up a jury rig. The hull itself had been racked by the sea. Captain Bentley wrote:

> 'The gun-deck standards lifted in the toes near two inches, and [I] am of the opinion the bolts are broke. The upper deck worked much in the same manner'.[40]

She returned across the Atlantic under jury sail arriving at Spithead on the 5th November. After a brief time in Portsmouth Dockyard for immediate repairs, she was ordered to be stored for Foreign Service on the 21st December.[41] She was certainly in no fit state to take part in the Second Louisbourg Expedition. Her weakened hull would explain why she succumbed so quickly to the grounding on the Horse Tail Sandbank.

Court Martial

The customary Court Martial, held when a ship is lost, took place on the 6th March onboard the *Royal George* in Portsmouth Harbour.[42] The last entry in Captain Bentley's *Journal of Proceedings*, now held in the National Archive,[43] reads:

> 'I, my Officers and the Whole Ship's Company where acquitted'.

The Admiralty Board were far from satisfied with the result asking Vice Admiral Holbourne, President at the Court Martial how it was possible that a large ship could be lost off Portsmouth with nobody 'blameable'.[44] Holbourne's reply does not read very convincingly, ending with the rather pathetic words:[45]

> 'This is the best account I can give for the loss of that ship'

On the 7th March, a second Court Martial was held for fifty sailors tried for 'Mutiny and Desertion'. It must have been an exhausting time for all onboard particularly the continuous task of manning the chain pumps. I suspect the charge may have been brought by a frustrated Bentley at this depressing time. The incident came about when the Ship's long boat had failed to return. The Court proceedings record:[46]

> '.. which they were prevented doing by wind and sea'

The sailors were all acquitted by the same Court Martial board. An unnamed Midshipman 'who was accidentally with them in the boat' was not charged.

Invincible's place on the Second Louisbourg Expedition was taken by the *Dublin*, the first of the new English 74s commanded by the future Admiral Sir George Rodney, and carried General Amherst to North America. Rodney had been one of the Captains on the Court Martial Boards that had acquitted Bentley and his sailors in the ship's long boat.

Captain John Bentley

Captain John Bentley (1703–1772)[47] had been Flag Captain to Admiral Lord Anson onboard the 90-gun *Prince George* when *L'Invincible* was captured in the First Battle off Finisterre in 1747. During this time, he had established a lasting friendship with Anson. Bentley, the second Captain of *Invincible* following her capture from the French, took command on the 8th December 1748 (Julian calendar date) until she was paid off on 15th November 1752 (Gregorian calendar date). This was equivalent to 4th November on the Julian calendar, the change having been made on 2–3 September 1752 by authority of the British Calendar Act of 1751.

Bentley's second command of *Invincible* was not a success. As previously described, the first expedition to capture the French Fortress in 1757 had resulted in the near loss of the ship off Cape Breton. On the Second Louisbourg Expedition she sadly failed to even leave The Solent.

Despite the loss of *Invincible*, Bentley continued to have a successful career. He was knighted on the 20th September 1759 after capturing the French 74-gun ship, *Téméraire*, at the Battle of Lagos Bay. She was the predecessor to British built '*The Fighting Temeraire*' immortalised by the painter Turner in 1839. He progressed up the Admirals' list ending as Vice-Admiral of the White on the 24th October 1770. On Friday, 3rd January 1772 he died and was buried at St Andrews Church, Buckland near his home in Kent.

Invincible's Records from 1758

There is a letter[48] dated 8th March 1758 from the Admiralty Office inviting the Navy Board:

'...to solicit the Lords Commissioners of His Majesty's Treasury for money to enable you to pay the officers and Ships Company the Wages due to them up to the day on which the said Court Martial was held, ...'

The letter goes on to say:

'And you are to dispense with the want of such Books of Accounts, Journals and other Papers as were lost with the Ship and cannot be delivered into the proper offices.'

The letter is signed: 'Your affectionate friends,
>Anson
>The Orby Hynalls
>I Forbes'

In fact, the Muster Book,[49] Captain John Bentley's journal of Proceedings from 30th April 1757 to the 6th March 1758,[50] and the Lieutenants' Logs did survive. The Lieutenants' logs make interesting reading. The day by day account of the disaster written by Robert Curry,[51] the Third Lieutenant, provides a realistic description of the attempts to refloat *Invincible*.

The Muster Book[52] lists the names of all officers, sailors and marines from the period 25th December 1756 to 6th March 1758. Each crew member was entered in order of joining. To find a person, a separate alphabetical index lists their names with their respective ship's book number; a few had more than one number after temporary discharges such as leave. The index was very necessary; there were twenty-four entries on every alternate page covering 1039 naval personnel and 225 marines during the 26 month commission. At any one time up to 29th April 1757 *Invincible*'s allowed complement was 715, and then reduced to 700 at the time of her loss. The complement included 100 marines and their officers. The Muster Book does not include Cornwallis's Regimental soldiers or other persons taking passage at the time of her wrecking.

The worry at the Admiralty Office about loss of documents does not seem to have caused any problems with the wage account. The Muster Book covering the commission was made up for each man's 'Full Wages'. These amounted to a total of £11,588 3s 7d before deductions: clothes (from slops and civilian contractors), beds, tobacco, Chatham chest, hospital, venereal cures and charges amounted to £1837 19s 5d. The accounts were approved by James Hubbold and William Oakley for the Treasury and by Philip Thomas and Richard Hogg for the Navy, and states:

'Paid in Broadstreet the 26th May following'

A few individual accounts are annotated to show that payment occurred some years afterwards. Interestingly, 'Net' wages are referred to as 'Neat' wages, the old English word for 'Net'.

Further examination of the Muster Book records 24 deserters marked 'R' who forfeited their wages and 40 naval fatalities marked 'DD' (discharged dead) during the commission. The latter's next-of-kin received their dues in most cases, but there appear to be a few others who never received their wages at all. The Marines had 15 deaths but no deserters.

The sorry saga of *Invincible*'s wrecking is officially recorded in Court Martial proceedings[53] starting with Captain Bentley's explanation of what went wrong, and his various answers to questions posed by the Board members. The Master, Mr Henry Adkins gave a lengthy explanation which collaborated Bentley's evidence. Other witnesses included: the two leadsmen, Thomas Gray and Thomas Francis; the Quartermaster, Thomas Moody; the Gunner, William Hook who had cleared the tiller rope when jammed; the Boatswain, John Fraser; and others. The final witness, William Locket the Dockyard pilot of 36 years standing, stated:

'the sand has increased more than I ever heard, or could imagine, and I should not have known there was so little water now, had I not gone out to the assistance of the Invincible when she was ashore.'

In the Court's findings, it refers to Locket 'the most experienced and best reputed pilot at the Port touching his knowledge of the Dean Sand'. It must have helped the Court decide that they:

'are unanimously of opinion that None of the officers are blameable for the loss of the Ship, and we do hereby acquit them of the same'

Other *Invincible* correspondence can be found in the Admiralty 'In and Out' letters.

Fisherman Arthur T. Mack recalls how he found *Invincible*

Arthur writes: "I have been interested in History since a young lad and these were the only lessons at school I was interested in. You could say my education was in the mud of Portsmouth Harbour where I was a mud lark.

"On the 10th June 1976 while trawling near the Fairway Buoy off the mouth of Langstone Harbour, I brought up in my net a pewter jug without a lid. I took it to show the Curator, Bill

Figure 15. Arthur Mack at the helm of his 16 foot Wishbone. Photograph John Broomhead.

Corney at Portsmouth City Museums. He sent it to the Honourable Pewter Company where it was recognised as being Dutch and a rare example from the early seventeenth century. A friend Dave Goften found in his trawl a similar jug in the same area. This prompted me to go looking for a possible seventeenth century wreck in that area but with no success.

"On the 5th May 1979, I was fishing with a good friend of mine Melvin Goften in his boat *Vanessa*. We were trawling on the Horse Tail sands in the Solent between Portsmouth and the Isle of Wight. That particular day the sea was flat calm and the land visibility excellent. After about an hour the boat came up with a tremendous jerk – the trawl had snagged on an obstruction on the seabed. The boat was pulled back over the obstruction; two turns were put on the samson posts with the warps. The boat was put in forward gear and the net was wrenched from the seabed and torn badly. In the net was a large square piece of timber; it had wooden treenails and very corroded iron bolts. Good transits were taken to avoid it another time.

"I took the timber home and became intrigued with it. I had a nagging feeling that there might be a very important wreck waiting to be found. I became so obsessed that I went out to the site with my own boat *Wishbone*. A chain was put between my two otter boards instead of a net and towed over the area. This was repeated for several days with no luck but I still had the gut feeling there was a wreck. On the 15th I found it, my persistence had paid off. An anchor and buoy was put on the wreck, I then retrieved my otter boards and went home. The next day I got in touch with a diver friend, John Broomhead along with Jim Boyle. We went out to the site in *Wishbone*, a fast west running tide was in full flow and the buoy had gone.

"Over the next two weeks I tried again and on the 28th 'bingo' I found it this time. I used a large anchor and buoy to mark the spot. That evening John and a friend came out to the site again and we took good landmark transits to find the site again. They then dived and confirmed there was a wreck but the visibility was not good but they did see large timbers protruding from the sand. They then removed the buoy and cleared the otter boards from the wreck. Over the next few months artefacts were brought to the surface and stored in wet rags to stop them drying out. I took photographs of them for my records.

"We contacted Alexander McKee asking what the wreck might be. He dived on the site which happened to be his 60th birthday; his opinion was that judging by the size of the wreck which was much bigger than the *Mary Rose*, it could be the *Impregnable*. There were reports of an old wreck in Hayling Bay – fishermen had torn their nets on an underwater obstruction. I had been given the transits at the time. In 1982 using the transits, I found the wreck which was later confirmed as the 98-gun *Impregnable* (1799) previously suggested by Alexander McKee. This wreck had been salvaged in Victorian times and her timbers can be found in the Impregnable Farm on Hayling Island.

"Our immediate problem was how to protect the site from pillaging by local divers. John Broomhead and I took my photographs of artefacts to Greg Clark, Curator of the Royal Naval Museum. He realised that this was an important wreck and put us in touch with Commander John Bingeman who was responsible for two of the wrecks off 'The Needles', the *Assurance* (1753) and *Pomone* (1811)."

Licensee's Involvement

That was how the *Invincible* wreck was first discovered and how I, the eventual licensee, became involved. As Arthur Mack has described, in March 1980 he and John Broomhead walked into my Portsmouth office and asked me to help them with a large wreck they had discovered. During that summer, they recovered seventeen artefacts hoping to identify the wreck but other divers had started pillaging the site. This threat prompted Arthur and John to seek further guidance by calling on Commander Gregory Clark at the Royal Naval Museum. I was well known to Commander Clark as his Museum already displayed artefacts from 'The Needles' wreck site where I had been excavating for the previous two years on behalf of the Isle of Wight Archaeological Committee directed by the County Archaeologist, Dr David Tomalin. This was the start of my rewarding and happy partnership with Arthur and John.

I was already committed to working the Needles wreck site as a Royal Naval Adventure Training Activity. It would be madness to get involved in another site. On the 4th April we all went out in MFV 119, the Portsmouth Royal Navy Sub-Aqua Club's 61½ foot diving tender, to see if this wreck was as outstanding as John Broomhead claimed. John took me round the site and I'm quoted as saying:

'John took me round the site and I was amazed with what I saw. The timbers went on for ever'

In fact, the site turned out to be 59 metres long. Any thought of not getting involved was quickly forgotten!

The identity of the wreck was unknown. As stated by Arthur, he and John had taken Alexander McKee, who found the *Mary Rose*, to dive the site. He suggested *Impregnable*, a 98-gun three decker lost in 1799. Subsequently, the remains of *Impregnable* were identified close inshore off Hayling Island.

What Ship?

In mid-September, while searching for clues at Portsmouth's Public Records Office,[54] I came across a reference to the loss of *Invincible*: 'running on a sandbank to the eastward of St Helens' with a date. I then checked the transcript of the *Invincible* Court Martial[55] held onboard the *Royal George* on the 6th March 1758; it confirmed the location as the 'Horse and Dean Sands'.

When meeting Arthur Mack and John Broomhead, I claimed that I knew the wreck's name but would keep it to myself until officially designated. Arthur and John kept pressing me but they never guessed her name despite me saying it was a famous ship and that they would be delighted with her identification! It was also important to keep the name secret as Southampton ITV (before the days of Meridian) had filmed us afloat on 4th September with the punch line: 'What ship?'

I kept telephoning the producer to screen the report as I was going public with her identification on the 30th September.

What a week! ITV screened our programme, which showed me jumping in without my DV (demand valve) in my mouth; it was only when I got to the bottom that I realised I needed air! The designation made the National TV. Keith Michelmore had made a great feature of not knowing her identity, only to express astonishment the next day announcing that it was the wreck of the Royal Navy's First *Invincible*. I was brought down to earth by receiving the 'Licence to Survey and Excavate' on condition that by the 22nd October, just a few days later, I must submit a full report 'on the progress of the survey and excavation operation'! I also had to complete a similar annual report on the excavations of HM Ships *Assurance* (1753) and *Pomone* (1811). It was a crazy time; I had a full time appointment as head of the experimental section at the Royal Navy's Nuclear, Biological and Chemical Defence School. I was also Chairman of the Royal Navy and Royal Marine Sub-Aqua Association with it's AGM on 10th October in London.

Identifying *Invincible*

Identifying the wreck was throwing up conflicting information; ordnance artefacts recovered indicated gun calibres of 9, 24 and 32-pounders whereas 74-gun ships at the time were armed with 9, 18 and 32-pounders. This difference in gun calibres raised the question as to whether the wreck was actually *Invincible*. Whilst studying Priddy's Hard Royal Armament Depot's archive in 1980, Dr David Houghton and I found various correspondence concerning *Invincible* among other ships. And then the breakthrough!

The letter (Fig. 16) dated 23 Dec 1755 from the 'Office of Ordnance' to the 'Respective officers at Portsmouth' ordered her '18 Pounders' to be changed to '24 Pounders'.[56] There was more correspondence about the size of *Invincible*'s gun ports 'for the New 24 Pounder Carriages'[57] besides the receipt dated 20th Feb'y 1756 acknowledging thirty 24-pounders from Woolwich delivered by the sloop *Hyam*.

Since Dr Houghton's and my visit in 1980, Priddy's Hard Royal Armament Depot has been closed down and the archive transferred to the Hampshire Records Office at Winchester. My photocopies of documents made in 1980 at Priddy's Hard were identified by Dr Anne Thick at Hampshire Records Office and their present day reference numbers have been used in this publication.

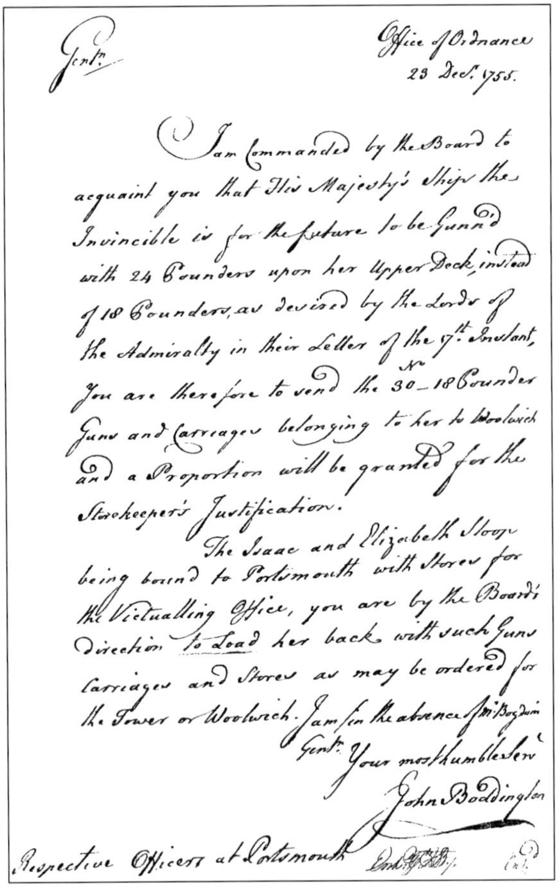

Positive identification of Invincible

On 30th May 1981 the Licensee, when excavating in the Forward Sail Room (its position is shown on the Orlop Deck plan in 'Appendix A'), found within a folded sail a tally stick (Figs 17 and 18) that finally removed any doubt as to the wreck's identification. At the time, Martin Woodward, owner of Bembridge Maritime Museum was diving with the Licensee and witnessed the find.

L'Invincible's *profile courtesy of Jean Boudriot*

Jean Boudriot, the author of the famous four volumes *Le Vaisseau de 74 Canons*,[59] provided photocopies of *L'Invincible*'s French plans. They were traced to improve their clarity and have been used extensively during *Invincible*'s excavations. They have also enhanced annual reports to the Advisory Committee on Historic Wreck Sites (ACHWS).

Figure 16. The letter from the 'Office of Ordnance' ordering the replacement of Invincible's *18-pounders with 24-pounders.*

Figure 17. Drawing by Peter Dawson.

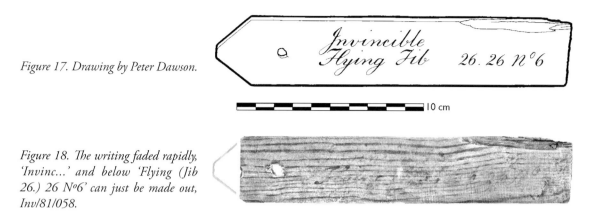

Figure 18. The writing faded rapidly, 'Invinc...' and below 'Flying (Jib 26.) 26 N°6' can just be made out, Inv/81/058.

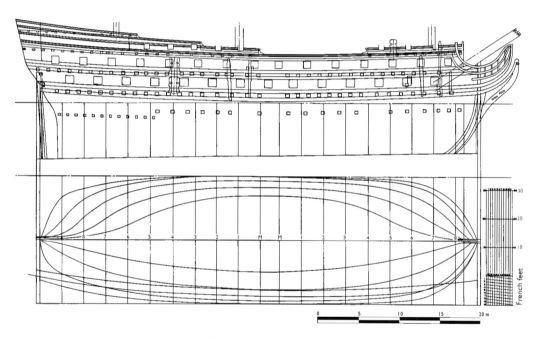

Figure 19. Tracing by Peter Dawson from L'Invincible's profile.

Survey following capture

The Admiralty, probably prompted by Admiral Lord Anson who had some expectation of Prize Money, ordered a survey of *Invincible* 'with all dispatch'.[60] The survey report, completed on the 14th August 1747, was signed by E. Collingwood, P. Lock, J. Lock, T. Bucknall, and T. Blankley.[61] The reason why so many senior shipwrights signed the report was probably because the survey included *Invincible's* valuation for a rather large sum of prize money. In fact, her total valuation was £26,139 18s 3d.

In the August 1747 survey over 200 iron knees were recorded. This must have been quite a surprise to the Survey team. The French had first introduced wrought iron knees into ship building in the

1720s due to the shortage of suitable timber. Two iron knees were recovered and one is examined in detail in Chapter 4. In the centre of the coherent hull structure shown on the 1998 final site plan (Fig. 62), there remains a group of three knees together; these are not in their original positions. There are likely to be more knees in the un-excavated areas.

Government site buoy

Laying our wreck buoy was another successful milestone. The Licensee had successfully lobbied the Department of Trade to fund our buoy. At the time there were 22 designated sites and this was only the second site to have a buoy, the *Mary Rose* being the first.

Figure 20. The buoy ready for laying. Photograph Peter Hales.

Figure 21. Laying the Invincible *wreck buoy, 31st March 1981. Left to right: The Licensee, HM Dockyard Portsmouth's mooring gang, John Broomhead. Photograph Peter Hales from Arthur Mack's fishing boat.*

The *Invincible* (1758) Committee

Jim Boyle, a friend of Arthur Mack and John Broomhead ran one of the local Diving Shops in Portsmouth and took part in early discussions. Shortly afterwards he moved his business to the West Country and later to Canada. From the Autumn of 1980, he ceased taking any interest in the Project.

By 1981, the Project – we called ourselves 'Invincible (1758) Committee' – had increased to five members. Dr David Houghton, Officer-in-Charge, Admiralty Exposure Trials Station, Eastney had taken a keen interest in our activities. He had allowed us to deposit a section of *Invincible*'s false keel at the Trials Station for safe keeping, and to place artefacts in his saltwater tanks prior to conservation. With the need for legal advice, Solicitor John Saulet was consulted and became fascinated with the Project and was our fifth member. Up to 1981, Portsmouth City Museums undertook artefact conservation. I had previously delivered all artefacts raised from the Needles Wreck site to the Museums' conservation facilities at French Street, Portsmouth.

We badly needed our own independent conservation facilities. Our Committee's decision was to form our own company: 'Invincible (1744–1758) Conservations Limited' with the five of us as directors. Simon Aked, a qualified Conservation Officer who had been working for Portsmouth City Museums Conservation Laboratory and had worked on conserving *Invincible*'s artefacts, agreed to work for our Company and later was invited to become a director.

With Simon the only full time member of the Company, we always had a manpower shortage, particularly as the rest of us were in full time employment. This was to remain the case until I retired from the Royal Navy after 36 years service at the end of 1986. Even so the Company's finances could only afford one full time member of staff, our Conservation Officer.

After setting up the Company, premises were bought at 6–10 Kirkstall Road, Southsea. Requiring a dry store for conserved artefacts, we also bought a small two storey building. In 1988, we moved the Conservation Laboratory to larger premises at Hilsea Lines in north Portsmouth.

Notes

1. NMM POR/D/9 dated 14 August 1747.
2. Hampshire Records Office, 109M91/CO12 dated 12 January 1747/8.
3. NA ADM 51/936, log of Strafford, 1/233, March 1745–6, Admiral's letters.
4. Duke of Bedford's correspondence, ed. Lord John Russell, London, 1842, 472.
5. *The Navy League Journal*, Vol. VIII No. 7, July 1903, Page 171.
6. Staffordshire Records Office D615/P(S)/1/9/22 and D615/P(S)/11/1.
7. BM Anson Correspondence Vol. II, 119.
8. Charnock, J. (1802) *An History of Marine Architecture*, Vol. III, 116.
9. NA ADM 95/25.
10. NA Admiralty 'Out' letter summary, 22 Jan 1747, 98.
11. Lavery, B. *The Royal Navy's First Invincible*, Portsmouth, 1988, 43.
12. NA ADM 95/25 f67.
13. Mountaine, W. *The Seaman's Vade-Mecum*, London, 1778, 18–19.
14. NA ADM 95/25, f67.
15. Staffordshire Record Office, D615/P(S)/1/9/22.
16. Naval Records Society, Vol. 131 British Naval Documents 1204–1960 – Memorandum from Sir John Williams, Surveyor of the Navy, to the King, 11 January 1774.
17. NA ADM 95/12 dated 21 May 1757.

18. Charnock, History of Maritime Architecture, London, 1800–2 Vol. III, 144.
19. Pritchard, J., From Shipwright to Naval Constructor: The Professionalization of 18th-Century French Naval Shipbuilders, *Society for the History of Technology*, Vol. 28(1987), 1–25.
20. *Ibid.*
21. Derrick, C. *Memoirs of the Rise and Progress of the Royal Navy*, London, 1806, 138.
22. *Barham Papers* 1, 9th April 1780, 325.
23. Hartland, J., *Seamanship in the Age of Sail*, Conway, London, 1984, 71.
24. NA ADM 95/12, 21 May 1757.
25. Spinney, D., *Rodney*, 1969, 132–9.
26. Hampshire Records Office: 109M91/CO15 – Office of Ordnance letter – Boddington to Respective Officers at Portsmouth dated 23 Dec 1755.
27. *London Magazine*, 1747, 258–9.
28. *The Gentleman's Magazine*, August 1755: XXV, 376 para H.
29. NMM, 1748/55: RUSI.
30. Hampshire Records Office: 109M91/CO15 – Office of Ordnance letter – Hartwell to Respective Officers at Portsmouth dated 23rd of Dec 1755.
31. NA ADM 2/219 – letter dated 21st October 1755.
32. NA ADM 1/5297.
33. WO 4/55 War office 'out' Letters, see 13 February 1758.
34. NA ADM 50/3 see Boscawen's proceedings for 19th February 1758.
35. *Ibid.*
36. Harper, J. R. *A Short History of the Old 78th Regiment (Fraser's Highlanders)*, DEV-SCO Publications, Canada, 1966, 42–3.
37. Harper, J. R. *A Short History of the Old 78th Regiment (Fraser's Highlanders)*, DEV-SCO Publications, Canada, 1966, 44.
38. NA ADM 1/5297.
39. NA ADM 50/3.
40. NA ADM 1/481 25th September 1757.
41. Office of Ordnance letter signed by W. Bogdani dated 21st December 1757.
42. NA ADM 1/5297 6th March 1758.
43. NA ADM 51/471.
44. NA ADM 2/522 "Out Leter 106" dated 8 March 1758.
45. NA ADM 1/926 dated 10th March 1758.
46. NA ADM 1/5297 7th March 1758.
47. Bentley, Richard. John Bentley, Knight, Vice-Admiral of the White, published privately, Guildford 1921.
48. NA ADM/A/2484 dated 8th March 1758.
49. NA ADM 32/96.
50. NA ADM 51//471.
51. NMM ADM/L/J/87.
52. NA ADM 32/96.
53. NA ADM 1/5297.
54. Gates, W. G., *History of Portsmouth*, 1931, Evening News and Hampshire Telegraph Company.
55. NA ADM 1/5297.
56. Hampshire Records Office, 109M91/CO15 dated 23 December 1755.
57. *Ibid.*
58. *Ibid.*
59. Boudriot, J., 1977 *Le Vaisseau de 74 Canons [The 74-gun Ship]* en quatre tômes, Collection Archéologie Navale Française, Paris France.
60. NA ADM/B/135 dated 8th June 1747.
61. NMM POR/D/9 dated 14th August 1747.

2. Publicity and Exhibitions. Publications. Funding and Staff. Diving. Artefact Policy

Publicity

The National Press take an interest

A 'square plate' was the artefact that caught the attention of the Press culminating in an article on the front page of the *The Guardian* for 23rd December 1980. Thanks to the help of an archaeological reporter, the late Miss D. Picton Jones, a number of short reports had appeared in local newspapers about the recovery of various artefacts.

Our first success at public relations

On 8th April 1981, Flag Officer Portsmouth, Rear Admiral Tippet opened our window display on the walkway to the Royal Naval Museum. The Museum had a similar display exhibiting artefacts recovered from 'The Needles' wreck site by my naval divers. The Museum's Director told me that 'The Needles' display

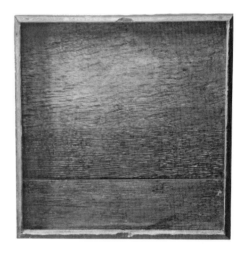

Figure 22. Square plate, Inv/80/236. From: Heart of Oak – A Sailors Life in Nelson's Navy by James P. McGuane. Copyright © 2002 by James P. McGuane. Used by permission of W. W. Norton and Company.

Old salts' square meals

By Alan Rusbridger

According to the Oxford English Dictionary, people began to have square meals around 1860 — but Commander John Bingeman, wreck explorer and serving naval officer, claims that square meals were eaten at least 100 years before then.

The dictionary's evidence is a series of American literary works in the 1860s which mention characters tucking into square meals. Commander Bingeman's evidence is four 12-inch square wooden plates he has recovered from the wreck of an eighteenth century warship in the Solent.

It is just a hunch, he admits, but it seems quite plausible to him that such artefacts should have been the origin of the exhortations of generations of mothers to be sure to eat three square meals a day.

"It suddenly struck me when we recovered these plates," he said yesterday. "It seems perfectly logical. Most of our sayings have a quite straightforward origin.

"Archaeologists tell me they have known of similar plates being found on land, but I don't think anyone has recovered them from a maritime situation before."

The plates, which have been salvaged from the 222-year-old wreck of the first HMS Invincible, are made of oak and three of them are in near-mint condition.

They have a beading around them of three eighths of an inch — known as a fiddle — to keep the food on the plate. On the base is engraved a broad arrow, signifying that they were government property. The plates are to go on display at the naval museum in Portsmouth next year.

HMS Invincible, built by the French in 1741 and captured by the English in 1747, sank in the Solent on February 19, 1758.

Figure 23. The Guardian for 23rd December 1980.

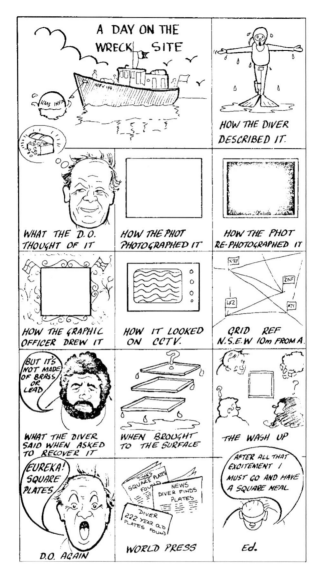

Figure 24. The Portsmouth Command Sub-Aqua Club newsletter saw it slightly differently! The Licensee confesses that he was also the Club's DO (Diving Officer). Drawn by John R. Terry.

had attracted considerable public interest over the previous two years and they were delighted to have the *Invincible* display.

I would like to record our thanks to the Royal Naval Museum for allowing us to have this public display following the discovery of the Royal Navy's First *Invincible's* wreck site. The new, sixth HMS *Invincible* had recently been commissioned so the timing of this discovery could not have been better. Thanks are also due to Chris O'Shea at Portsmouth Museums Conservation Laboratory for the conservation of the artefacts displayed; and to John Terry, one of our divers and a gifted artist who painted the scene of *Invincible's* stranding on that fateful Sunday morning on 19th February 1758 (see

Figure 25. The window display at the Royal Naval Museum.

the cover). The sandglass, top right is the only item which is not genuine; it is a replica of the half-hour sandglass (Inv/79/013) made by Roger Trise. The original was considered too delicate for the window display.

Archaeological symposium

The Archaeological Symposium at Fort Bovisand in March 1982 gave us the first opportunity to tell the greater archaeological world about Protected Wreck Site Number 22. We put together a table display, and I was invited to give a 30 minute presentation about the wreck site.

Further presentations were given at the Fort Bovisand Symposiums during the following years. The Licensee has continued to give lectures about *Invincible* to various organisations

Figure 26. The opening ceremony. Left to right: Captain Livesay (CO of the 6th HMS Invincible*), John Terry (the artist), Arthur Mack (finder of the wreck site), Admiral Tippet (Flag Officer Portsmouth), John Broomhead and Licensee. Photograph Peter Hales.*

Figure 27. Some of the early artefacts recovered, with a copy of John Terry's oil painting of Invincible *aground. Salt glazed jug, cartridge cartouche, fid, gunner's primer handle (metal spike lost by corrosion), 30-minute sandglass, miniature barrel, gun flints, small rigging block, hand grenade, square plate and a 9lb rammer head. Photograph Peter Hales.*

mainly in Hampshire and Sussex, but occasionally further afield. These have been given in aid of the Royal National Lifeboat Institution (RNLI).

The Invincible *1744–1758 bus*

John Broomhead organised our own exhibition bus, which often proved a real money earner for the Project. On the near-side it was fitted with glass show cases, and behind the driver's seat there was a sales desk. Among the items for sale were musket shot in presentation boxes, pieces of tarred rope (its smell was the attraction), rope mounted on *Invincible* oak, a whole range of monogrammed clothing, as well as a booklet giving *Invincible's* history, the excavation site plan and illustrations of artefacts recovered. Takings at Portsmouth Navy Days could exceed £3,000 over the three days.

To achieve these good sales, it was essential to have members of the diving team present. On other occasions when we had volunteers not directly involved with diving, takings would barely cover the entry fee to the event.

Figure 28. Our bus at Portsmouth Navy Days alongside HMS Invincible. *Photograph Jane Bingeman.*

Figure 29. English Heritage funded a display board close to Southsea Castle overlooking the Invincible *wreck site – Arthur Mack with the Licensee. Picture courtesy of* The News, *Portsmouth.*

Exhibitions

'Wooden Walls' exhibition

Chatham Dockyard built their exhibition 'Wooden Walls' in the Old Mast House which includes the Mould Loft on the top floor. This was a most appropriate building since it dated back to the middle of the 18th century. The exhibition's theme is the building of *Valiant* seen through the eyes of William Crockwell who joined the Royal Dockyard in 1757 apprenticed to John North, the shipwright. *Valiant* at Chatham, and *Triumph* at Woolwich, were ordered to be built to *Invincible*'s lines 'notwithstanding any orders to the contrary'.[1]

Figure 30. Chatham Historic Dockyard Mast House and Mould Loft.

The Admiralty had previously paid *Invincible* her greatest compliment describing her as: 'in every respect the best ship of her class and answers all purposes that can be desired of a ship of war'.[2] Of further interest, the Chatham Mould Loft was used for HMS *Victory*'s moulds following *Valiant*'s completion in 1759.

Travelling exhibition

In 1984, the Project set up a travelling exhibition for hire. It was first exhibited at the Hospitality Inn, Southsea and was opened by the pop singer Robin Gibb from the "Bee Gees". A hundred guests from the archaeological world, museums, and some members of the Advisory Committee on Historic Wreck Sites including their Secretary, Ian Milligan were present. Chichester District Museum was the first to hire the exhibition. The exhibition included a fifteen-minute continuous video tape showing diving on the site.

Figure 31. One of the exhibition display cases with Invincible*'s artefacts.*

Figure 32. View of the exhibition panels.

Figures 33 and 34. Two of the six show cases.

Exhibitions abroad

During the Autumn of 1981, Portsmouth City Museums' painting exhibition at the Museum der Deutschen in Duisburg-Ruhrort, Germany borrowed recently excavated artefacts from the *Invincible* wreck site to augment their exhibits. The *Mary Rose* Trust also lent artefacts.

For a period of four months in 1986 during the Canadian Trade Fair, the Vancouver Museum was lent thirty-five artefacts for their exhibition 'Captain George Vancouver – A Voyage of Discovery'. They wanted contemporary items to support their displays. Simon Aked, *Invincible*'s Conservation Officer, was funded by the Canadian authorities to attend the Trade Fair and help set up the exhibition.

Publications

Interim report

The *International Journal of Nautical Archaeology*[3] published a short paper written by the Licensee introducing excavations that were taking place on this recently protected wreck site. Much of the paper has been incorporated into this book and has been enhanced by further research that has become available since 1984.

Gunlocks: their introduction to the Navy

The Licensee gave a paper at the British Naval Armaments Conference held at the Royal Armouries in November 1987.[4] In 1756 *Invincible* had been selected as one of thirteen ships to try out cannon locks on her 9-pounder Quarterdeck guns.[5] While no locks have been recovered, other allied gunnery equipment like 'Aprons of Lead' and large cannon lock flints were discussed. The Licensee compared these finds with his earlier work based on recoveries at 'The Needles' off the Isle of Wight from the *Pomone* (1811) wreck. These included a cannon lock by 'W. Dick' and a special 'Apron of Lead' with a 'hump' to accommodate a mounted cannon lock (see Figs 226 and 227 for Aprons, and 228, 229 and 230 for locks).

Book: 'The Royal Navy's First Invincible'

Brian Lavery had so impressed us with his book *The Ship of the Line* in two volumes, that we invited him to write the definitive book about *Invincible* and our excavations. Brian took on the task, researching the archives at Paris and Rochefort where *Invincible* had been built and we made available all our own research information. Brian produced an excellent manuscript published by our company in 1988.[6] A total of 1000 hardback and 1000 paperback books were printed and these have all been sold.

Conference: 'The Archaeology of Ships of War'

The Licensee read a paper at the two-day Greenwich Conference on *The Archaeology of Ships of War* on the 31st October/1st November 1992 sponsored by various maritime organisations including the National Maritime Museum. The paper[7] was based on the more unusual recoveries from the *Invincible* wreck site, and the Project's contribution to Nautical Archaeology.

Funding and Staff

Funding

The artefacts recovered up to 1981 had been released by the Receiver of Wreck to the Licensee. Some of these released artefacts were valued for J. Saulet Esq. (the Project's Solicitor), by W. H. Lane and Son, Valuers and Fine Art Auctioneers at Plymouth to establish a value for funding purposes, but not for sale. The Valuers had previous experience selling similar artefacts recovered from wrecks in the West Country and the Isles of Scilly. Their Certificate of Valuation dated 25th August 1982, valued the artefacts at £23,755. On the strength of this valuation, the Midland Bank advanced monies for the Project to fund itself. The Licensee, absent due his duties during the 1982 Falklands War, only subsequently became aware of this arrangement. Later that year he joined the other Project members in signing individual Bank guarantees for the loan to finance a Conservation Laboratory.

Staff

We only had one full-time employee, the Conservation Officer, Simon Aked; the rest of us all held down full time jobs and worked voluntarily in our spare time. Our greatest problem was finding the manpower to run everything from conservation to setting up the Travelling Exhibition country wide.

Diving

Up to 1986, all the diving was carried out by volunteers; firstly from the Naval Sub-Aqua Club's MFV, and from 1984, in the Project's 25 foot workboat *Ceres*, fitted with a small LP (low pressure) air compressor and a HP (high pressure) Dunlop air compressor for the diving cylinders. This was replaced in 1986 by *Viney Peglar* (Fig. 35), a 40 foot ex-pilot cutter bought by the Licensee. He fitted a Broomwade 80 cubic foot LP air compressor which was capable of driving two four inch air lifts. The Project bought a new diesel powered Bauer 7 cubic foot HP diving air compressor.

Diving conditions

At peak spring tides, the low water depth was 5.5m and high water 10m. Diving during these periods was avoided as the tidal stream reached 1.8 knots. These periods were identified by high water being in excess of 4.4m above Chart Datum. This limited the maximum depth of diving operations to just over 9m making the site very diver friendly. The Board of Trade limit of four hours per day for air diving was followed.

An interesting situation arose when depth gauges recording maximum depths indicated well over two metres above the actual true depth. The explanation turned out to be the occasional Channel ferries' wake that created a long swell travelling across the site. These peaks were ignored. Perhaps technically they should have limited bottom time but no divers' bends were experienced during the eleven years of excavations. The regular divers would spend close on two hours underwater and have a brief break before returning for a second session. This system worked well.

Summer sea conditions in the 1980s in 'The Solent' were more tranquil than they became in the early 21st century. The site was tenable in westerly winds up to Force 5 since the site was largely protected by the Isle of Wight. From the East and particularly South-East it was a different story and at times even a Force 4 could be marginal. South-East winds had an added disadvantage; they stirred up the sands and destroyed underwater visibility, though visibility seemed to marginally improve when using an airlift. The divers needed at least half a metre's visibility for safe excavation.

The tidal stream was basically either westerly or easterly, while the site was spread in a line from north-west to south-east. The tide running either way was generally sufficient to carry the airlift deposits clear of the trench under excavation. The Licensee made a regular check of the air lift deposit scatter looking for the occasional small artefact carried over. The diving workboat was normally a fairly stable platform, but there were periods when the

Figure 35. Viney Peglar, *the Licensee's Workboat – Arthur Mack is on the right pointing at the photographer. The white line in the foreground is the air hose. Photograph John Broomhead.*

tide changed and with a cross wind, the situation could be described as interesting! We kept going.

Viney Peglar was previously a pilot cutter at Avonmouth, and named by Mrs Viney Peglar whose husband was the Chairman of the Bristol Pilotage Authority. Mr Peglar later became Lord Mayor of Bristol.

Artefact Policy

What to do with the artefacts?

In Chapter 3 under 'Conservation', we recorded months of discussions with Portsmouth Museums Service for an agreement. The Royal Naval Museum's Director took part in these talks chaired by the Director of Portsmouth Museums. The talks failed. Portsmouth's proposals were unacceptable, and the Royal Naval Museum declined to accept the artefact collection. This was sad since *Invincible,* following her capture from the French, had always been a Portsmouth ship. Her artefacts would have provided a complementary link between the *Mary Rose* (1510–45) and *Victory* (1768). The Director of Chatham Historic Dockyard Trust, General Sir Stuart Pringle, Royal Marines, welcomed us.

Chatham Historic Dockyard Trust

In January 1988, after months of negotiation, an agreement was signed between Chatham Historic Dockyard Trust and the *Invincible* Project. The Trust would select at least one of every type of artefact so far recovered. This would form the basis of 'The Representative Collection' which would be developed at the end of each diving season. In return, Chatham Dockyard would pay £25,000 towards the Project for the next three years helping to cover the cost of conservation. Today the collection at Chatham consists of 680 artefact entries, some entries covering more than one example of the same artefact, e.g. there are 35 galley bricks.

Christie's sale of artefacts

The Project was re-financed in September 1987, by various individuals who had become interested in the Project. This still left a significant shortfall for the future. The Directors agreed that if we were to continue, surplus duplicate artefacts not required by Chatham Historic Dockyard, could be sold. Christie's South Kensington Limited was approached, and they agreed to hold a unique sale of *Invincible*'s artefacts on the 10th March 1988.[8]

The Licensee with his accountant brother-in-law calculated that the Project would need to raise at least £100,000 to give it a viable future. The sale raised around £64,000. We had a serious shortfall with likely financial problems ahead.

The ethics of selling artefacts

Since the early days of the Project we had been selling a few of the 12,000 musket shot in presentation boxes, and short lengths of tarred rope (with that glorious aroma) mounted on a piece of *Invincible* oak.

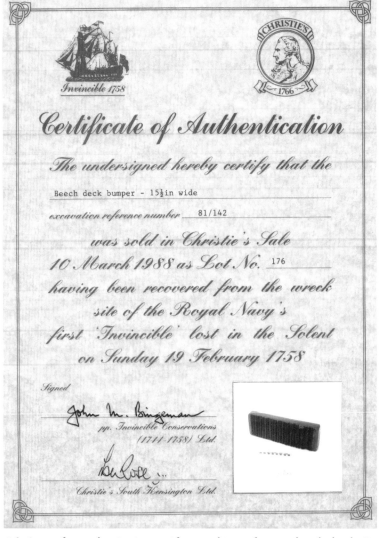

Figure 36. An artefact authentication certificate – this artefact was bought by the Licensee.

In view of the large quantities recovered this seemed harmless, particularly given the precedents from various land excavations, including the sale of surplus Roman nails from an historic site in the north.

The Christie's sale created the more serious ethical problem of selling significant artefacts. My background as a Naval Officer has taught me to apply common sense to all situations. The ideal would have been to keep all the finds together until the Project was complete; realistically, however, the large quantities of identical artefacts and the financial pressures led to a compromise. We had already set up the agreement with Chatham Historic Dockyard Trust for their Curator to have first pick each year of all artefacts and take at least one of every type. So reluctantly I agreed with my fellow Directors that Christie's sale should go ahead. Legally, we were the owners of the artefacts cleared by the Receiver of Wreck. The Project was within the law to sell all or any of the artefacts. We felt our consciences were clear to go ahead with the sale.

We hoped that many of the objects would be displayed in their historical context since several groups of finds were purchased by museums in this country and Australia. The Tower of London, the Shipwreck Heritage Centre at Hastings, and subsequently the Royal Naval Museum at Portsmouth has been among the buyers.

To many people, what we did was archaeological heresy. Today with more stringent Government controls administered by English Heritage, similar excavations and artefact disposal would not be allowed. However, the sale enabled us to complete the excavation of *Invincible's* coherent hull structure, and contribute extensive research which has been of wide-ranging benefit to Nautical Archaeology, all on a very low budget.

Authentication certificates

Each of the 298 items auctioned at *Christie's South Kensington Limited* on the 10th March 1988 had an Authentication Certificate to confirm the artefact's origin signed by the Licensee on behalf of *Invincible Conservations (1744–1758) Limited* and by Tom Rose, Associate Director of Christie's. Figure 36 is a copy of one of the 298 certificates raised.

Management problems

Three Directors, Simon Aked, John Broomhead and John Saulet had ambitious plans for the Company which in the Licensee's opinion were not justified. Out-voted, the Licensee resigned his Directorship of 'Invincible Conservations (1744–1758) Limited' following the Christie's Sale in March 1988, and withdrew his Bank guarantee. However, he remained the site's Licensee and continued to play a full part working for the Company with responsibility for: diving, annual reports to ACHWS, and reporting artefacts recovered to the Receiver of Wreck. The Company ceased trading in 1991 and went into voluntary liquidation. The remaining Directors were responsible for the debts following the Company's liquidation. John Broomhead volunteered to dispose of the Company's assets on behalf of the Midland Bank, the major creditor, on the understanding that this would offset against his full personal liability as a Director. The majority of the Company's assets were duplicate artefacts not required by Chatham Historic Dockyard Trust. Initially, John, with a friend, set up the first *Invincible* website (www.wgarrett.demon.co.uk) to sell artefacts and replicas. This was subsequently replaced by John's own site www.invincible1758.co.uk. John eventually cleared his personal liability with the Midland Bank (now HSBC) and the unsold artefacts remained in his possession for sale.

Invincible *websites*

For the record, the Licensee was never consulted about, nor approved of, the internet sales and has never had any connection with either of the two *Invincible* websites.

Invincible *Project post-1991*

The Licensee has personally funded all diving, with the help of Arthur Mack, since 1991 to the present. He has also funded professional drawings of artefacts, research and reports leading up to writing this Final Report titled *The First HMS Invincible*. The Licensee has given numerous lectures about *Invincible* and recently includes five of the other six historic protected wreck sites in 'The Solent' – this excludes the *Mary Rose*. Money received for these lectures have been donated to the RNLI. Dr Margaret Rule was for the first 11 years the site's Archaeological Director. Since the licence has been reduced from excavation to survey, she has continued as the Site's Archaeological Advisor. Margaret has never received any remuneration.

Notes

1. NA ADM 95/12, 21 May 1757.
2. *Ibid.*
3. *International Journal of Nautical Archaeology*, (1985), 14.3: 191–210.
4. Smith, R. D. ed. (1989), *British Naval Armaments*, Royal Armouries, London, 41–44.
5. NA ADM 2/219
6. Lavery, B. (1988) *The Royal Navy's First Invincible, Invincible Conservations (1744–1758)* Limited, Portsmouth, UK.
7. Mensum, B. (ed.), *Excavating Ships of War, Vol. 2*, 168–176, Anthony Nelson, England 1998.
8. Christie's South Kensington Limited, Catalogue ref: 'SHIP 2700' dated 10 March 1988.

3. Early Survey and Designation. Conservation. Survey and Excavations

Early Survey

Getting involved

How do you go about excavating a large wreck site? Arthur Mack, John Broomhead, Jim Boyle and I were in full agreement that we must apply for a Government Protection Order. This would designate the wreck as a protected site ensuring that it was worked to an acceptable archaeological standard. In May 1980, I as Chairman and Diving Officer of the Portsmouth RN Sub-Aqua Club (previously HMS Vernon SAC – BSAC Branch 749) was able to undertake a pre-disturbance survey as a Naval Adventure Training activity. My team of young sailors tackled the task enthusiastically and it is satisfying to know that their 1980 pre-disturbance survey was to prove surprisingly accurate when compared to a second survey by professional archaeologists in 1984/5.

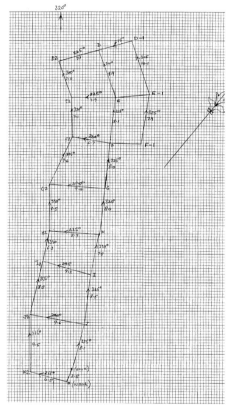

Figure 37. Jackstays, measurements and orientation for the 1980 pre-disturbance survey – each small graph paper 'square' represents 0.5m² – measured and drawn by Norman Bradburn.

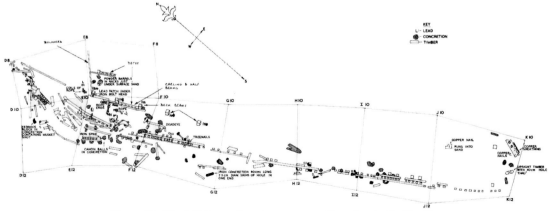

Figure 38. The 1980 pre-disturbance survey. Site plan by B. Tomkins.

Designation

With the pre-disturbance survey complete, I was able to submit the application form in time for the July 1980 meeting of the Advisory Committee on Historic Wreck Sites (ACHWS) under the chairmanship of Viscount Runciman of Doxford. While deeply involved with the excavation of the *Mary Rose*, Dr Margaret Rule, CBE FSA had kindly consented to take on the additional responsibility of the site's Archaeological Director. Christopher O'Shea, Curator of Conservation at Portsmouth City Museums agreed to continue to be responsible for conservation. The application was successful. I had the advantage of 'learning the trade' when diving on the *Mary Rose* in the 1970s, followed by two years experience leading work on the Needles Wreck site on behalf of the Isle of Wight Archaeological Committee. I was aware of the formalities involved in running a Protected Wreck site. My second advantage was that the ACHWS knew my track record from my annual reports submitted for 'The Needles' Wreck site [HM Ships *Assurance* (1753) and *Pomone* (1811)].

While our application for designation had been accepted by the ACHWS, we now had to wait four weeks following the Public Notice in the press. This would give time for any objections before the Statutory Instrument could be laid before Parliament.

There were no objections, and the Statutory Instrument passed into law on the 30th September 1980 signed by Norman Tebbit on behalf of the Department of Trade.

It was a proud moment for Arthur Mack, John Broomhead and me to achieve this designation

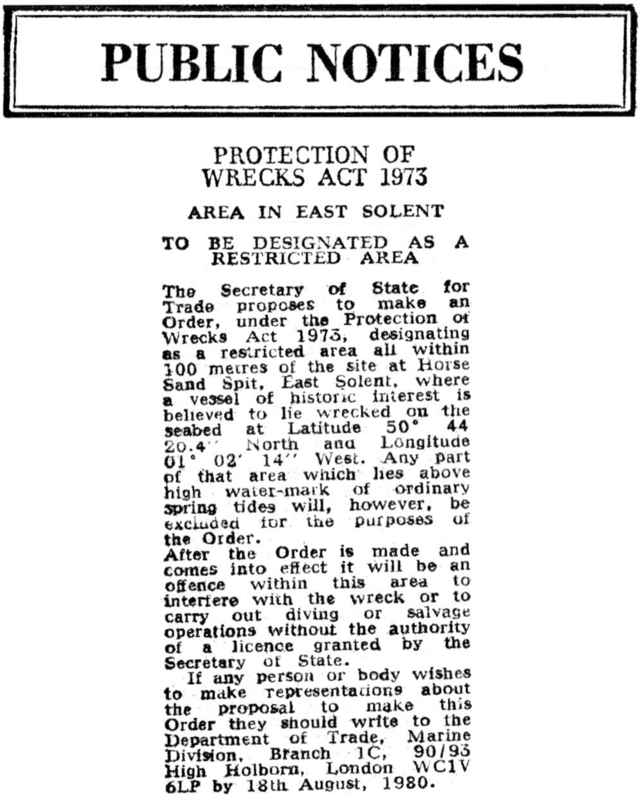

PUBLIC NOTICES

PROTECTION OF WRECKS ACT 1973

AREA IN EAST SOLENT

TO BE DESIGNATED AS A RESTRICTED AREA

The Secretary of State for Trade proposes to make an Order, under the Protection of Wrecks Act 1973, designating as a restricted area all within 100 metres of the site at Horse Sand Spit, East Solent, where a vessel of historic interest is believed to lie wrecked on the seabed at Latitude 50° 44 20.4″ North and Longitude 01° 02′ 14″ West. Any part of that area which lies above high water-mark of ordinary spring tides will, however, be excluded for the purposes of the Order.

After the Order is made and comes into effect it will be an offence within this area to interfere with the wreck or to carry out diving or salvage operations without the authority of a licence granted by the Secretary of State.

If any person or body wishes to make representations about the proposal to make this Order they should write to the Department of Trade, Marine Division, Branch 1C, 90/93 High Holborn, London WC1V 6LP by 18th August, 1980.

Figure 39. The Daily Telegraph, *Wednesday, July 30 1980.*

on the 30th September 1980 – only the 22nd site to be so honoured by the 1973 Act of Parliament to protect our Underwater Heritage. It was particularly poignant to have been the project leader for this Designation Order and to become the Government's Licensee, never previously achieved by a serving Naval Officer. I would like to record our thanks to Dr Margaret Rule for her guidance throughout the excavations. Since the completion of the excavations, she has remained the site's archaeological advisor to the present day.

Figure 40. Dr Margaret Rule, the site's archaeologist. Photograph Peter Hales.

STATUTORY INSTRUMENTS

1980 No. 1307

PROTECTION OF WRECKS

The Protection of Wrecks (Designation No. 2) Order 1980

Made - - - -	*1st September* 1980
Laid before Parliament	*9th September* 1980
Coming into Operation	*30th September* 1980

The Secretary of State, being satisfied that the site identified in Article 2 of this Order is, or may prove to be, the site of a vessel believed lying wrecked on or in the sea bed and that on account of the historical and archaeological importance of the vessel the site ought to be protected from unauthorised interference, after consulting with the persons referred to in section 1(4) of the Protection of Wrecks Act 1973**(a)**, in exercise of the powers conferred upon him by section 1(1), (2) and (4) of that Act and all other powers enabling him in that behalf, hereby orders as follows:—

1. This Order may be cited as the Protection of Wrecks (Designation No. 2) Order 1980 and shall come into operation on 30th September 1980.

2.—(1) The site in respect of which this Order is made is hereby identified as the site where a vessel lies, or may prove to lie, wrecked on or in the sea bed at Latitude 50° 44.34′ North, Longitude 01° 02.23′ West.

(2) The area within a distance of 100 metres of Latitude 50° 44.34′ North, Longitude 01° 02.23′ West, but excluding any part of that area which lies above high-water mark of ordinary spring tides, shall be a restricted area for the purposes of the Protection of Wrecks Act 1973.

Norman Tebbit,
Parliamentary Under-Secretary of State,
1st September 1980.   Department of Trade.

EXPLANATORY NOTE
(*This Note is not part of the Order.*)

This Order designates as a restricted area for the purposes of the Protection of Wrecks Act 1973 an area in the East Solent round the site of what is, or may prove to be, the wreck of a vessel which is of historical and archaeological importance.

(a) 1973 c. 33.

Printed in England by Harrison & Sons (London) Ltd., and published by Her Majesty's Stationery Office

835/32419   L.76   K8   9/80

30p net

ISBN 0 11 007307 X

Figure 41. Statutory Instrument.

Excavation policy

The first question following the award of a 'license to excavate' was 'what should be our policy'. The *Mary Rose* (launched in 1510) had set the precedent when the whole hull was raised after removal of its contents. This was because little was known about Tudor shipbuilding. The situation with *Invincible* (launched in 1744) was different. Her draughts were still held by the French in Paris and a full survey report had been carried out at Portsmouth shortly after her capture in 1747.[1] So there was little or no archaeological justification for lifting what remained of her hull.

In consultation with Dr Margaret Rule, the site's Archaeological Director, it was decided to record the hull structure after recovering the contents lying within the coherent hull. At this stage only a few artefacts exposed by the falling seabed had been recovered to prevent them being swept away. These artefacts aroused considerable interest as *Victory* (laid down at Chatham in 1759) would have carried similar items when first commissioned.

Conservation

Artefacts

A working relationship with Chris O'Shea, Conservation Officer for the City of Portsmouth Museums Service in French Street, Old Portsmouth already existed. Since 1978, on behalf of the Isle of Wight Archaeological Committee, I had been bringing Chris artefacts from the *Assurance* (1753) and *Pomone* (1811) lying on the scattered wreck site at 'The Needles'. Chris now undertook conservation of the few *Invincible* artefacts lifted in 1979 and 1980 while the future of the Project was under discussion.

We next approached Portsmouth Museums Service to discuss the future of the *Invincible* Project under their auspices. Over a period of six months a series of meetings took place with Richard Harrison, Director of the Portsmouth Museums to consider a suitable joint *modus operandi* for the Project. Some of these meetings were also attended by other interested parties including Captain Ray Parsons, the Director of the Royal Naval Museum, and his deputy, Commander Greg Clark; by Mr Len Mitchell, Head of the Isle of Wight Museums and Libraries with his County Archaeologist, Dr David Tomalin. We were hopeful that the *Invincible* artefact collection could become a substantial feature in a local museum. Already in April 1981, a window display had been set up on the public walkway to *Victory* with an eye catching oil painting by John Terry depicting *Invincible* aground buffeted by heavy seas – see cover and Figure 26. The display had been unveiled by Flag Officer Portsmouth, Rear Admiral Tippet with around twenty artefacts drawing one's attention to their remarkable state of preservation. Disappointingly, Captain Parsons, Director of the Royal Naval Museum, turned down further collaboration between the Project and the Naval Museum.

This surprised us since we were offering a considerable 18th century archive of authentic artefacts to enhance *Victory*'s restoration to her 1805 condition. Twenty years later, *Victory*'s Curator, Peter Goodwin took on a selection of artefacts from *Invincible*. If the decision had been made earlier the collection available would have been far larger. Peter also used many of *Invincible*'s artefacts as patterns for a whole range of replicas such as square plates, wooden bowls, tankards on the mess decks, and a range of ordnance stores including the hanging magazine framing, cartridge cases and powder barrels.

The *Invincible* Committee and Portsmouth City Museums failed to agree an acceptable joint *modus operandi*. The Museum's conditions were: a budget of £100 a year to support the diving operation; they would fund and be responsible for all conservation; and retain ownership of the artefacts subject to the usual clearance by the Receiver of Wreck. It seemed that after all our hard work in establishing the wreck site and achieving its designation, we would lose all control over the future of the *Invincible* Project except the responsibility for the diving. We also suspected that with our drive and leadership taken away, the Project would come to a standstill allowing the main emphasis to be directed towards the *Mary Rose*. It seemed that Portsmouth Museums' proposition was contrary to the spirit of the 1973 Protection of Wrecks Act which encourages the finders to play a full part in the future of any historic wreck site.

Perhaps rather rashly, in 1982 the *Invincible* Committee decided (with the help of John Saulet, a Solicitor who had been engaged by the civilian members of the Committee without remuneration) to form 'Invincible (1744–1758) Conservations Limited'. We set up our own company to excavate the historic wreck site backed by its own conservation department. Simon Aked, a recently qualified conservation officer working for Portsmouth Museums Conservation Department agreed to join our company and set up a laboratory in Southsea. We were fortunate that we were able to buy premises previously used by the Serck Radiator repair agent which included many of the facilities needed for a laboratory. These premises served us well until we moved to larger ones at Hilsea in 1989. After excavation was completed, the 'Invincible (1744–1758) Conservations Limited' company was wound up in 1991.

Going back to 1982, the *Invincible* Project was now independent and could proceed with our agreed policy of hull contents recovery and recording the hull structures. Our annual reports kept the Advisory Committee on Historic Wreck Sites apprised of our plans, facilities for working the site and artefacts' conservation. These arrangements were endorsed by the annual issue of licenses to excavate the site up to 1990 when we completed the policy task set in 1981. Since then, the Licensee has received a 'survey' licence to monitor the site annually.

Looking back, our team of six made a remarkable contribution to nautical archaeology without public finance or appeals. It is one of the few sites that has published a definitive book, *The Royal Navy's First Invincible*,[2] as well as annual reports, various articles and papers in the *International Journal of Nautical Archaeology* including the *Dating of Military Buttons*[3] (reproduced at Appendix B) whose evidence was described by the Deputy Director of the National Army Museum as 'electrifying'!

Invincible *conservation laboratory*

'Invincible Conservations (1744–1758) Limited' ran our conservation laboratory (Figs 42 to 44) at Portsmouth from 1983 until 1990. Prior to this our conservation had been undertaken by Portsmouth City Museums in their French Street Laboratory under the direction of Christopher O'Shea. Our ferrous conservation, mainly hand grenades and shot, continued to be treated in their hydrogen reduction furnace.

Figure 42. Laboratory Reception. Simon Aked, the Conservation Officer and Arthur Mack.

Figures 43 and 44. One of the conservation freezers and a treatment tank.

Surveys and Excavations

Diary of surveys and excavations

Following the award of the Government Excavation licence, the excavations took place over ten years. The following list should help clarify what happened over these years.

1981 Trenches: these were numbered 'A' to 'D' and were in part re-opened again in 1983 and 1984.

1982 No excavations. Licensee involved with Falkland War administration at the Ministry of Defence in London.

1983–4 Trenches 'A' to 'D' were re-opened to complete excavations.

1985 Repeat pre-disturbance survey and small exploratory trench in the stern area, see Figure 53 for isometric view of trench.

1986 Two 10m × 5m square trenches labelled 'North 86 and South 86'. These two trenches were emptied of artefacts.

1987 Four 5m × 5m square trenches labelled '87' split into 'NW, NE, SE, and SW' were completely cleared of artefacts.

1988 Six 5m × 5m square trenches labelled '88A to 88F' were completely cleared of artefacts. Trench 'Δ88' ('Triangle 88') previously opened in 1981 was re-opened as it was known to contain artefacts.

1989 Twenty 5m × 5m square trenches labelled 'G to Z' were excavated. Trenches 'P, R, Y and Z' were not completely cleared due to collapsed heavy timbers illustrated in the 1998 composite site plan (Fig. 62).

1990 Seven slightly larger trenches labelled 'AA, BB, etc to JJ' were dug. These were comparatively shallow trenches revealing large timbers thought to have originated from the collapsed transom and stern structures.

Pre-disturbance surveys, 1980 and 1984/5

The first pre-disturbance survey was carried out in 1980. The method used was fairly rudimentary using rope jackstays secured to half metre iron stakes hammered into the seabed on either side of what appeared to be a coherent hull structure. Underwater visibility in May was reasonable and by triangulation the 'squares' were plotted accurately. The team, mainly young sailors untrained in archaeology, were able with guidance to measure and draw the features in each of the 'squares'. This formed the basis for our recording until 1984.

In 1984, Dr Margaret Rule, the site's archaeological director, decided that a further detailed survey was required. This would include the previously unrecorded detached timbers lying to the north-east of the coherent hull structure. The second survey was carried out by Alex Hildred, Barrie Andrian (Burden), Ian Oxley and the Licensee. It was completed by the middle of the 1985 season. The earlier exploratory trenches dug close to the ship's bow had been backfilled, so to all intents and purposes the new survey could be considered as a second pre-disturbance survey. Considerably more timbers of the coherent hull structure were now visible as the seabed had lowered approximately 0.25 metres since the 1980 survey. For the next five years the seabed level continued to drop slowly, possibly caused by erosion as thousands of tons of ballast were being dredged daily east of the wreck site. After 1990 the seabed remained static, and more recently the level has risen back to above the 1980 level. But there is little doubt that dredging in the 1980s threatened the stability of the site.

The 1984/5 survey used prominent hull features marked with white Formica tallies as datum points. These datum points on prominent hull timbers were subject to both gribble worm attack and erosion in subsequent years. However, they did last long enough for accurate datum points to be re-established each season. To improve accuracy, temporary datum points were placed to augment hull structure datum points so that triangulations could be repeated.

The second pre-disturbance survey was divided into two parts:

a. The coherent hull structure survey of 1984/5. The divers' drawings were generally to a scale of 1:10 easily verified by knowing the exact distance between the seventy datum points located on each of the exposed port side hull timbers. The Licensee then reduced these slightly varying scales, using a photocopier with a percentage adjustment capability, down to an exact scale of 1:50 before tracing them on to a master permatrace sheet 1.2 metres long.

b. The 'detached timbers' survey of 1984. On the 20th August 1984 using a similar 1:50 scale, Ian Oxley completed the co-ordination of the individual surveys made by himself, Alex Hildred, Barrie Andrian and the Licensee. The Licensee then related this plan to the master site plan.

Hull orientation

During the excavations of 1985, an investigative trench at the southern end of the site revealed that what we had for sometime thought was the bow was in fact the stern. This showed that we had been using an incorrect hull orientation.

How had this happened? On the copies of *L'Invincible*'s plans, kindly sent to us from Paris by Jean Boudriot, the ship's store rooms were marked near the stern. On the early exposure of a store room in 1981 we had therefore assumed that we were working near the stern. What we had not known was that *Invincible*'s store rooms had since been repositioned nearer the bow, probably by the Royal Navy during the four-year refit in Portsmouth (1752–56).

To further confuse us, the adjacent exposure of a keel rider marked 'CXIIII' (see Fig. 45) had, by its high number, supported the idea that we must be near the stern. We had not appreciated that French naval architecture is based around the positions midship beam ('maitre bau') and the associated midship frame ('maitre couple') at the widest part of the ship. They are used as the key to a numbering system that extends both fore and aft. Thus a number 'CXIIII' can occur at both bow and stern. What we had found was in fact the number near the bow.

Put simply, our early site plans had been drawn the wrong way round. All original drawings from that period have since been amended for this publication and now show the correct orientation of the hull.

1981 excavations

Figure 45 shows the exploratory trench dug in 1981. The keel rider knee marked 'CXIIII' was revealed for the first time, giving rise to the belief that such a high number must be near the stern. Subsequent study of the French plans show the numbering started at the hull centre (maitre bau) and going both forward and aft, thus explaining why 'CXIIII' can also be found at the bow.

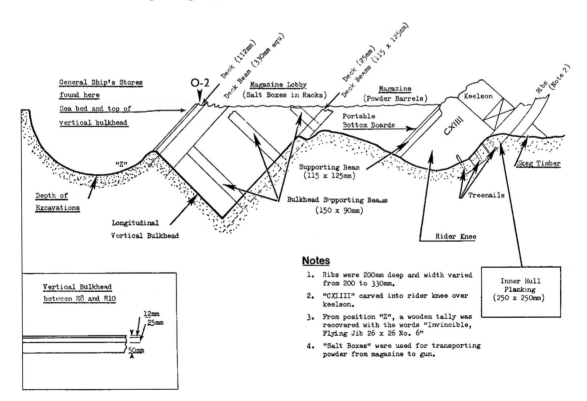

Figure 45. Exploratory trench dug in 1981. Drawing John Bingeman.

1982 excavations

Although the 'Advisory Committee on Historic Wreck Sites' had granted a licence for the 1982 Season, no excavations were undertaken. The Licensee, a serving Naval Officer, was unavailable, working full time at the Ministry of Defence in London during the Falklands War. Arthur Mack and John Broomhead continued to monitor the site. Sixteen artefacts exposed on the surface were recovered to prevent their loss.

1983–4 excavations

Extensive excavations took place during the 1983–4 seasons and many hundreds of artefacts were recovered. These excavations were followed by making drawings of the exposed hull's port side.

Figures 46 and 47 show the 1983–4 excavations that featured in the 1984 Annual Report to

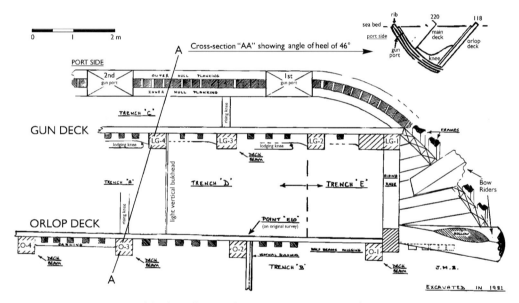

Figure 46. Plan of 1983–4 excavations. Drawing John Bingeman.

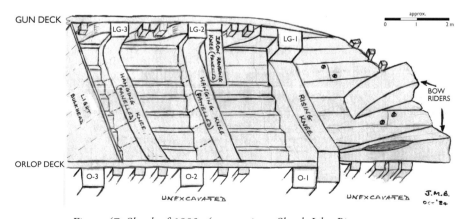

Figure 47. Sketch of 1983–4 excavations. Sketch John Bingeman.

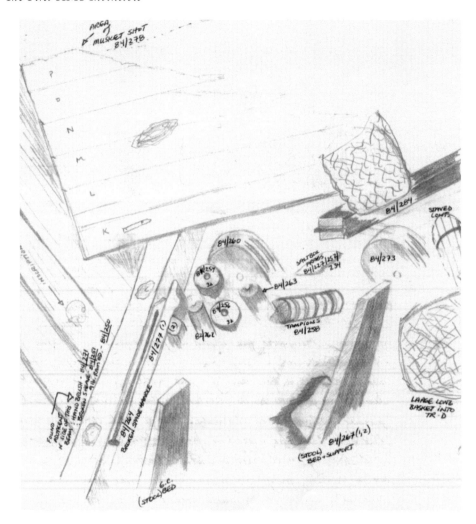

Figure 48. View of trench being excavated. From Barrie L. Andrian's diving report dated 24th June 1984.

ACHWS. A typical scene while a trench was being excavated is shown in a drawing (Fig. 48) by Barrie Andrian when she took over an air lift to excavate trench 'E'. Datum points had been established at seabed level to measure the position of artefacts before recovery.

Part of the on going excavations carried out in 1983–4 is illustrated in Figure 49, which shows an area on the Gun Deck around the second gun port.

Figure 50 provides a clear idea of *Invincible*'s port side hull structure from the second gun port on the Gun deck down to the Orlop deck. It complements Figure 51, which shows the store room sketch on an even keel, whereas the ship actually lies at an angle of 46°. What is not apparent is that the Orlop deck's rising knee ('O-4') or 'Standard' is actually made of wrought iron hidden underneath pine wood panelling (see later discussion of iron knees in Chapter 4).

The drawing by Ian Oxley (Fig. 52) shows the same area at its actual angle of 46° and was drawn three days before the sketch in Figure 51.

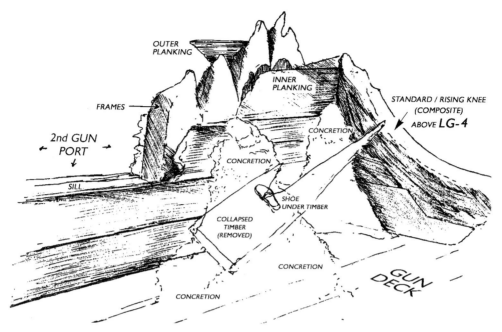

OUTER
PLANKING

INNER
PLANKING

FRAMES

STANDARD / RISING KNEE
(COMPOSITE)
ABOVE *LG-4*

2nd GUN
PORT

CONCRETION

CONCRETION

SILL

SHOE
UNDER TIMBER

COLLAPSED
TIMBER
(REMOVED)

CONCRETION

GUN
DECK

CONCRETION

Figure 49. View of excavations in progress. Sketch Jonathan R. Adams.

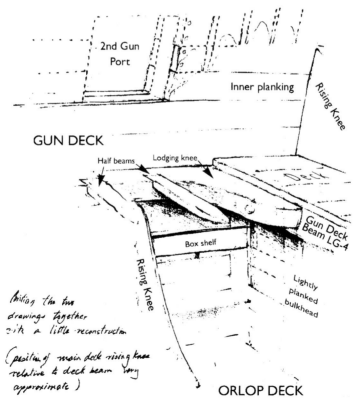

2nd Gun
Port

Inner planking

Rising Knee

GUN DECK

Half beams

Lodging knee

Deck

Gun Deck
Beam LG-4

Box shelf

Rising Knee

Lightly
planked
bulkhead

*Position the two
drawings together
with a little reconstruction*

*(position of main deck rising knee
relative to deck beam very
approximate)*

ORLOP DECK

Figure 50. Hull structure above and below the Gun deck. Sketch Jonathan R. Adams.

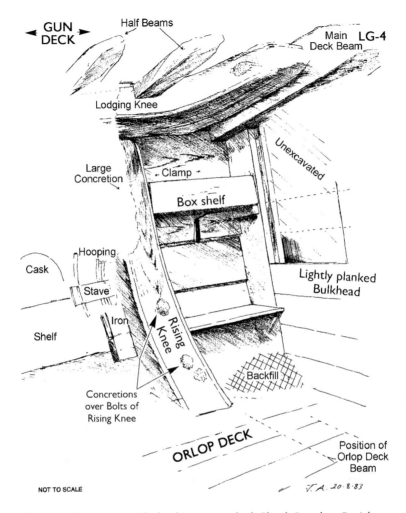

Figure 51. Store room with the ship on even keel. Sketch Jonathan R. Adams.

1985 survey and stern excavations

The majority of the 1985 season was spent repeating the 1980 pre-disturbance survey, with particular reference to what are called 'the detached timbers' lying mainly to the north-east of the coherent hull structure. These are mainly the starboard side separated from the main hull during *Invincible's* break up and a few sections of decking.

A small investigative trench was dug just forward of the stern post and included the aft gun port on the Gun deck. The isometric sketch (Fig. 53) shows a top frame timber (labelled 19) above the gun port which became detached during the excavation. The sketch includes the shattered end of the 4.13m section of false keel (top right) lying on the sea bed referred to later in this Chapter and shown complete on the site plan in Figure 59.

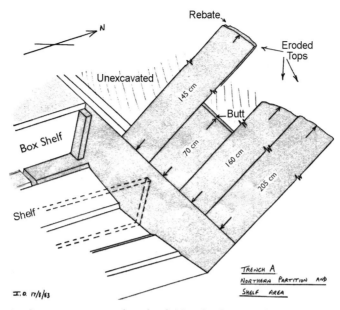

Figure 52. Store room at actual angle of 46°. Sketch Ian Oxley, 17th August 1983.

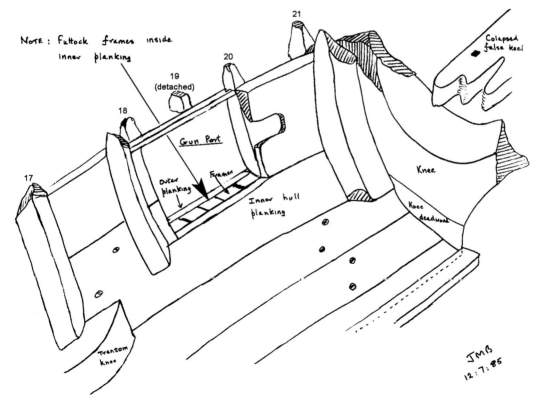

Figure 53. Isometric view of the 1985 stern excavations. Drawing John Bingeman.

Typical drawings made during excavations

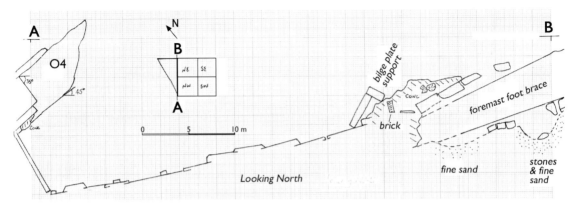

Figure 54. Hull cross-section from Orlop main deck beam O-4 towards Invincible's *keel looking forward. Drawing David Burden, 1987.*

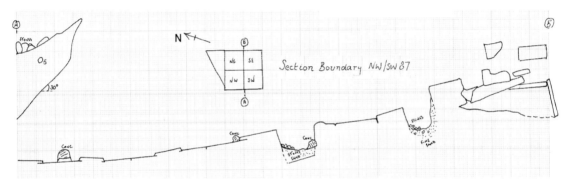

Figure 55. Hull cross-section from Orlop main deck beam 'O-5' up to the first futtock looking forward. Drawing David Burden, 1987.

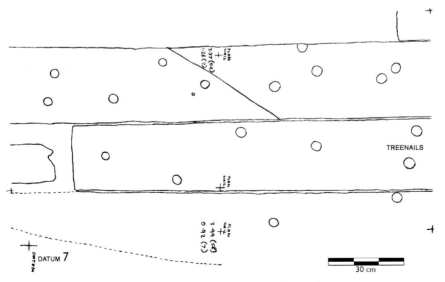

Figure 56. Original drawing 1:10 – the deck planks are 12 inches wide. Drawing Louise McDonagh.

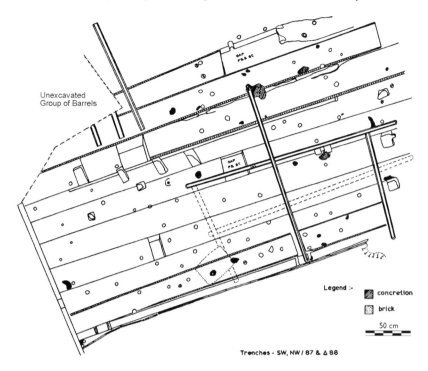

Unexcavated
Group of Barrels

Legend :-

▨ concretion

▨ brick

50 cm

Trenches - SW, NW / 87 & △ 88

Figure 57. Hull drawings were compiled in small sections before placing within a 'Collector' plan. Drawing Robert Stewart.

Survey methodology

When each trench was emptied, a survey of the hull structure was carried out using a metre square frame subdivided into 10cm squares. A half-metre square as seen in Figure 58 was also used, if more appropriate, in restricted corners.

Site plan following the second pre-disturbance survey

On completion of the second pre-disturbance survey, the site plan of the coherent hull (Fig. 59) was drawn by the Licensee. The numerous measurements and datum points from the survey are omitted to improve clarity. The visible surface features are identified to improve recognition of the salient features. The datum points used are shown and analysed in Figure 70 by Nick Rule using his Direct Survey Method (DSM).

Figure 58. Chris Underwood recording the hull structure using a half metre square. Photograph Chris Dobbs.

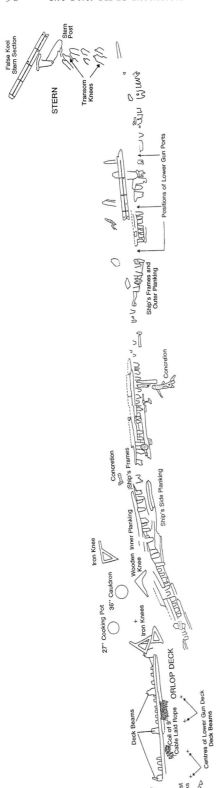

Figure 59. Site plan of the coherent wreckage following the second pre-disturbance survey.

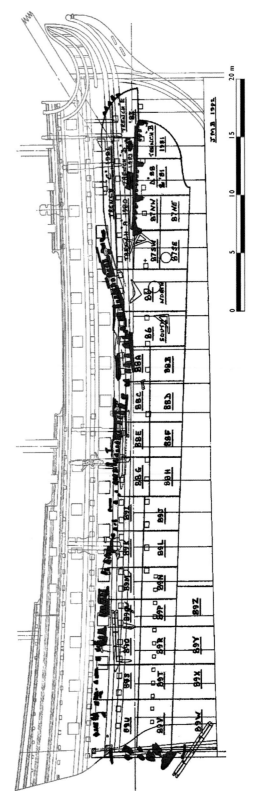

Figure 60. Invincible's profile with exposed hull timbers superimposed.

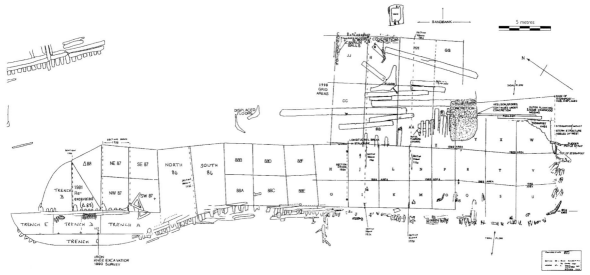

Figure 61. The 1990 drawing of trenches with timbers exposed during excavations that year.

Invincible's profile with exposed hull timbers superimposed

The purpose of Figure 60 is to marry the second pre-disturbance survey (1984–5) with the hull profile. Also shown are the excavation trenches (1981–90) with their respective identification. It will be seen that the initial trench identifications were superseded by a more standard system using a letter and the last two digits of the year when a trench was opened up.

Hull survey

Between 1986 and 1990, the coherent hull was excavated section by section from bow to stern. After excavation and recording of the artefacts lying in each section, individual drawings were made of the exposed hull before backfilling. These hull drawings were finally collated by the Licensee in 1998, and his work re-traced by Norman Lacey to produce a fair copy (Fig. 62) – scale 1:50.

Figures 63 and 64 of underwater sketches made five days apart in August 1989 provide a clear idea of the solid state of the hull that had been sealed beneath the seabed. Figure 64 shows the port hull planking and transom knees.

Sonar scan

In May 1995, the University of Southampton's vessel was on a north-easterly course while passing over the centre of *Invincible*'s coherent hull structure and recorded the side- scan sonograph (Fig. 65).

An interpretation of Invincible's break up

Following her stranding in 1758, *Invincible* dug herself only a shallow grave despite her displacement of 1826 tons. This was due to the fact that she lay on top of a comparatively solid shingle bank

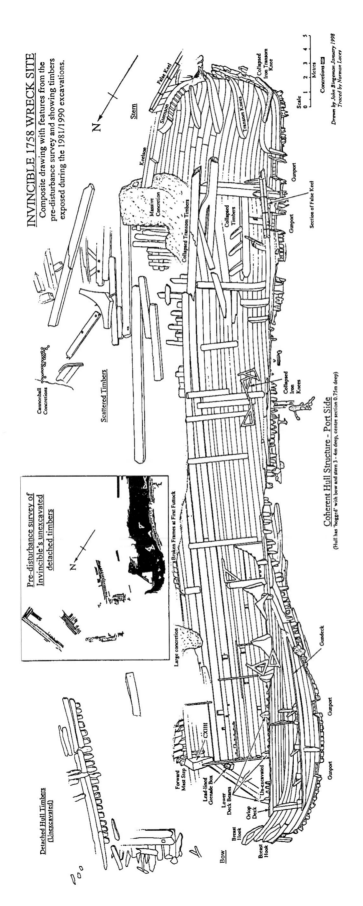

INVINCIBLE 1758 WRECK SITE

Composite drawing with features from the pre-disturbance survey and showing timbers exposed during the 1981/1990 excavations.

N

Stem

Cannonball Concretions

Scattered Timbers

False Keel

Sternson

Kerlson

Massive Concretion

Collapsed Transom Timbers

Transom Knees

Collapsed Iron Transom Knee

Collapsed Timbers

Gunport

Gunport

Section of False Keel

Scale
0 1 2 3 4 5
Meters

Concretions

Drawn by John Bingeman January 1998
Traced by Norman Lacey

Collapsed Iron Knees

Coherent Hull Structure - Port Side
(Hull has 'hogged' with bow and stern 3 - 4m deep, centre section 0.75m deep)

Detached Hull Timbers
(Unexcavated)

Pre-disturbance survey of Invincible's unexcavated detached timbers

N

Large concretion

Broken Frames at First Futtock

Bow

Breast Hook

Breast Hook

Forward Mast Step

Lead-lined Grenade Box

Lower Deck Beams

Orlop Deck

Un-excavated

CXIIII

Gunport

Gundeck

Gunport

Figure 62. The 1998 composite site plan. Drawing John Bingeman, traced by Norman C. Lacey.

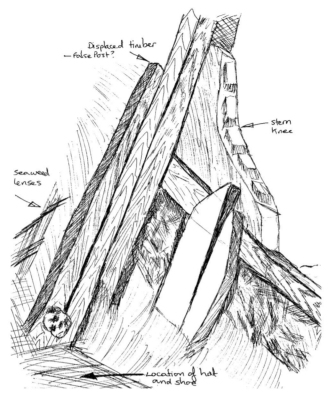

Figure 63. From Damien Sanders' diving report dated 2 August 1989.

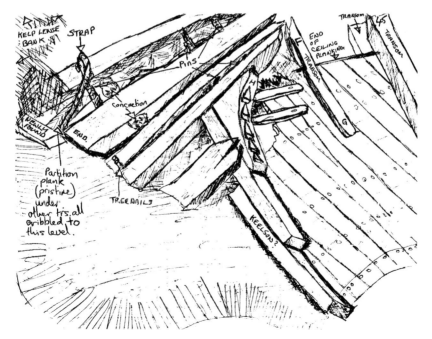

Figure 64. From Damien Sanders' diving report dated 7 August 1989.

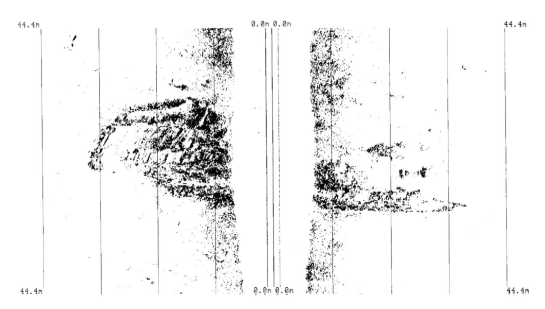

Figure 65. A side-scan sonograph trace of Invincible's *wreck site.*

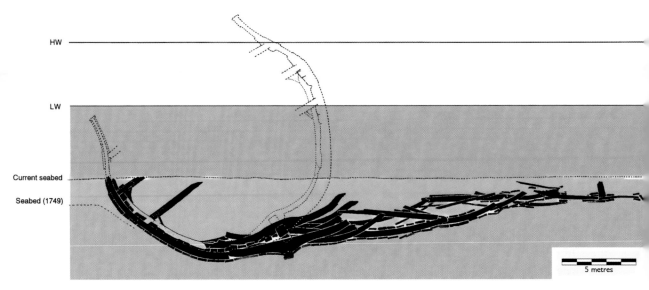

Figure 66. Jonathan R. Adams' interpretation of Invincible's *break up.*

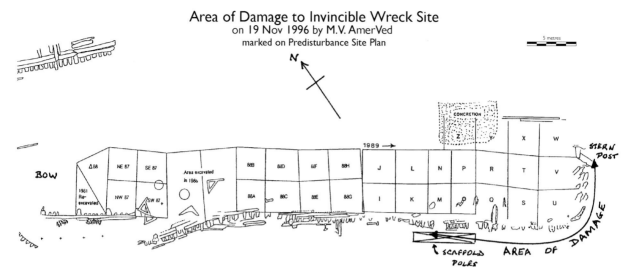

Figure 67. Enclosure to Licensee's letter dated 10/12/96 to ACHWS.

preventing her hull achieving a deeper penetration of the seabed. The *Mary Rose*, on the other hand, sank in water nearly twice as deep into soft mud and much of her hull was safely cocooned within the seabed. She also lay in a slightly more protected area within 'The Solent' while *Invincible*, lying on the Horse Sand Spit, was more exposed to southerly and south-easterly storms. The break-up of timbers are spread from south-west to north-east.

Severe damage to the site

On the 19th November 1996, the merchantman MV AMER VED's engine failed and she went aground within the *Invincible* protected area. On the following day at high tide in preparation for towing, she snagged and hoisted the wreck buoy complete with sinker, while recovering her anchor.

Damage had occurred over a length of 25 metres. *Invincible*'s 1½ metre high stern post had disappeared and has never been seen again. Substantial timbers over a metre long were lying loose on the seabed. Iron knees had lost their concretion covering and a broken section of iron knee was lying loose. A pile of scaffold poles previously used when working the site had been partly scattered.

The incident was immediately reported to the Secretary of the Advisory Committee on Historic Wreck Sites, Department for Culture, Media and Sport. After my site inspection, a full report dated the 10th December 1996 was sent to the Secretary. It is understood that no action was taken against the owners of the AMER VED after she was towed to Southampton Docks for repairs.

The Department of Oceanography at the Southampton Oceanography Centre had carried out a side-scan sonograph survey in 1995 and repeated this survey in August 1997. The second survey clearly shows the absence of previously indicated timbers following the grounding of the AMER VED.[5]

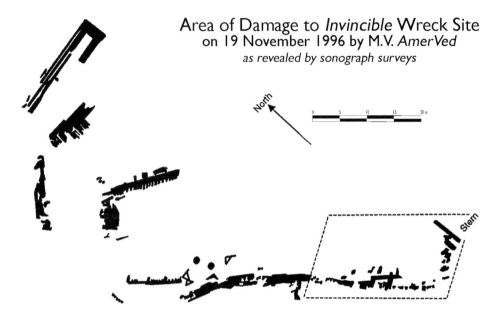

Area of Damage to *Invincible* Wreck Site
on 19 November 1996 by M.V. *AmerVed*
as revealed by sonograph surveys

Figure 68. The Oceanography survey in August 1997. Illustration Rory Quinn.

Wessex Archaeology 2003 multibeam image

In 2003 Wessex Archaeology was commissioned by English Heritage to undertake a Designated Site Assessment of the *Invincible*.[6] The inspection included a multibeam sonar survey of the whole site with the Licensee's site plan super-imposed (Fig. 69, p. 64). The multibeam image shows the accuracy of the individual survey blocks, but their relationship with each other is less accurate. This is no surprise to the Licensee; their relationship had depended upon long distance measurement with tapes in limited underwater visibility.

Area 'A' is the coherent hull structure which was excavated between 1980 and 1990. Areas 'B, C and D' have been referred to as the 'detached timbers' and they remain un-excavated today. This survey took place after the damage to the site by the grounding of the AMER VED on the 19th November 1996 which destroyed 25 metres of the visible stern timbers.

Direct Survey Method analysis of datum points

During the eleven years of excavating this large site, it became necessary to have a series of datum points to support the particular area being worked. Nick Rule's Direct Survey Method analysis looked at the relationship of 542 measurements. The result was an average residual error of 25mm, after seventeen measurements were discounted because of excessive error.

The visual presentation (Fig. 70, p. 65) shows measurements in colour. Green had an accuracy of within 20mm, with the blue and red being less accurate. Colour density of the lines increased as the error increased.

The less accurate red and blue measurements correlate with the Wessex Archaeology scan which showed that the north-east timbers were not tied into the main coherent structure as accurately as one would have liked. Remember that these longish distances were measured in limited underwater visibility and within a tidal stream that bows the measuring tape.

The licensee is most grateful to Nick Rule for this important contribution to the Project and for all the major work involved.

Notes

1. NMM POR/D/9 dated 14 August 1747.
2. Lavery, B. 1888 *The Royal Navy's First Invincible*, Invincible Conservations (1744–1758) Limited, Portsmouth.
3. *The International Journal of Nautical Arcaheology* (1997) 26.1: 39–50.
4. International Journal of Nautical Archaeology (1998) 27.2: 136.
5. International Journal of Nautical Archaeology (1998) 27.2. 126–138. *The* Invincible *(1758) site – an integrated geophysical assessment.* Rory Quinn, Jonathan R. Adams, Justin K. Dix, Jonathan M. Bull.
6. Wessex Archaeology Report Ref: 53111.03g dated January 2004.

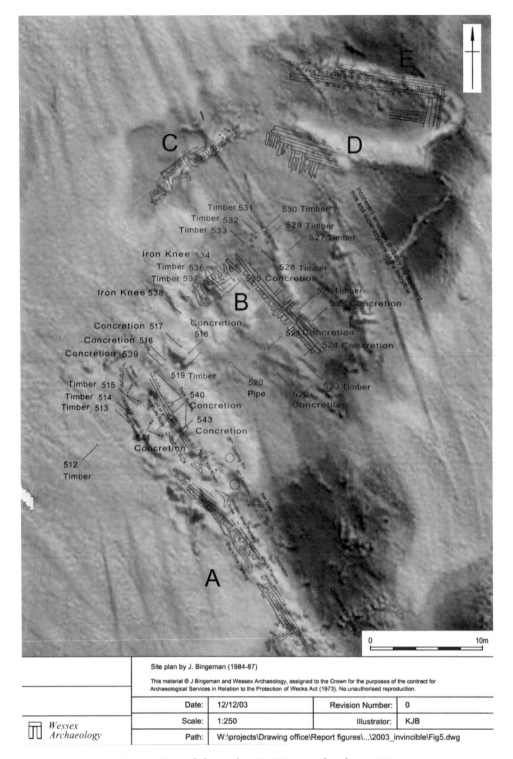

Iron Knee 534
Timber 536
Timber 537
Iron Knee 538
Timber 531
Timber 532
Timber 533
530 Timber
529 Timber
527 Timber
528 Timber
535 Concretion
526 Timber
525 Concretion
521 Concretion
524 Concretion
Concretion 517
Concretion 516
Concretion 539
Concretion 518
519 Timber
520 Pipe
522 Concretion
523 Timber
Timber 515
Timber 514
Timber 513
540 Concretion
543 Concretion
541 Concretion
512 Timber

Site plan by J. Bingeman (1984-87)

This material © J Bingeman and Wessex Archaeology, assigned to the Crown for the purposes of the contract for Archaeological Services in Relation to the Protection of Wecks Act (1973). No unauthorised reproduction.

	Date:	12/12/03	Revision Number:	0
Wessex Archaeology	Scale:	1:250	Illustrator:	KJB
	Path:	W:\projects\Drawing office\Report figures\...\2003_invincible\Fig5.dwg		

Figure 69. Multibeam data © Wessex Archaeology 2003.

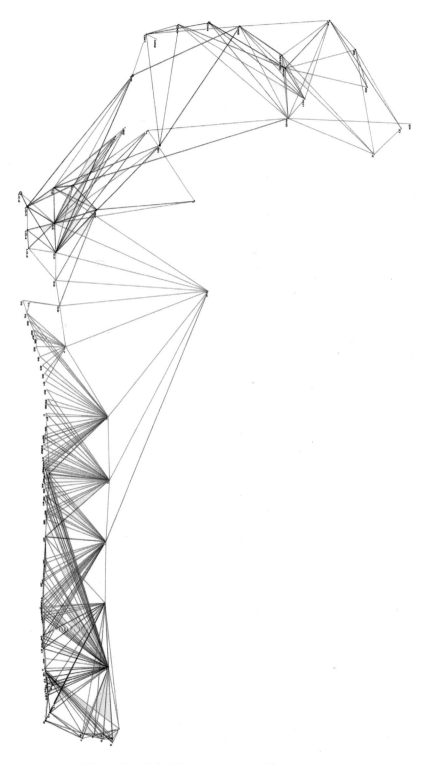

Figure 70. Nick Rule's presentation of datum points.

4. The Ship. Rigging, Ropes and Cables. Navigation

The Ship

Hull timbers

During the many years of excavation, the hull structure was left intact. Only loose timbers like carlings and the odd loose section of deck beam were recovered.

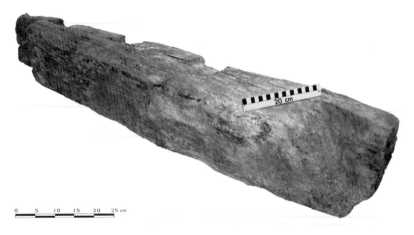

Figure 71. An oak carling from the bow area with slots to accommodate half-deck beams. Dimensions: 1470 × 230 × 210mm. Photograph John Bingeman.

Figure 72 is a typical example of a loose oak timber found lying on the seabed whose purpose and position were not established. It measured 1000 × 250 × 180mm and had three treenails.

Figure 72. A typical oak timber. Photograph John Bingeman.

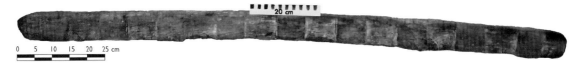

Figure 73. Upper deck grating piece: 1580 × 85 × 75 mm with ten slots for right angle strips, material oak. Each slot contained the traces of two nail holes. Photograph John Bingeman.

Timber marks

When ships were built, shipwrights used timber marks to help with construction. These marks could vary from a simple line to a formal numbering system. The most specific mark was found on the keel rider near *Invincible*'s bow marked 'CXIIII', see Figure 45. The following simpler marks on the inner hull planking are shown in Figures 74 and 75.

Figure 74. A timber mark on the Orlop deck inner hull planking. Scale bar measures 20cm. Photograph Chris Dobbs.

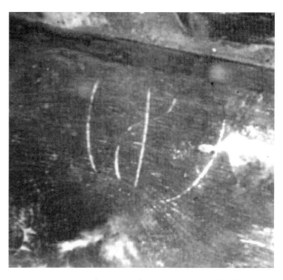

Figure 75. Timber mark on inner hull planking. Photograph Chris Dobbs.

Treenails

Several treenails were found in the hull timbers, as seen in Figures 76 and 77. Some of their 1½ inch diameter heads were found to be marked by 'squares', as Figure 78 illustrates. My first impression was that these treenails had square plugs in their centre. Closer examination showed the shape to be formed by four chisel splits, each containing a piece of caulking (Fig. 79). The purpose was presumably to expand the outside of the treenail and thereby prevent leakage. It is interesting to compare (Fig. 78) the square arrangements found on treenails from *Invincible*, launched in 1744 at Rochefort, France, with the triangular arrangement used on a similarly sized treenail found on a discarded oak timber from HMS *Victory* launched in 1768, all being caulked for the same purpose. There is, however, no certainty that any of these oak treenails were part of those ships' original hull structures.

Figure 76. Invincible's *timber length 1.171m – treenails had 'squares'. Oak timber, Inv/88–T3 – NE Trench.*

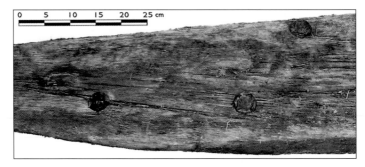

Figure 77. Close up of Fig.76 showing 'squares'. Both photographs John Bingeman.

Figure 78. Oak treenails. Both diameters 1½ inches (38mm). Photographs John Bingeman.

Figure 79. Caulking removed from one of Invincible's *square treenail heads. Photograph John Bingeman.*

False keels

False keels were fitted to protect ships' hulls for two purposes. Firstly, as a sacrificial timber to protect the main keel against damage; and secondly, by increasing the ship's draft, it would reduce the amount of leeway under sail.[1] These keels were usually made of a softer wood than the oak used for the main keel; and were made up in approximately 5m sections extending the full length of the hull.

Three sections of false keel were visible close to the surface on the seabed. The two similar elm keel pieces at the stern are shown in Figure 80; the third piece, Figure 83, at the bow had closely packed copper nails covering the whole surface.

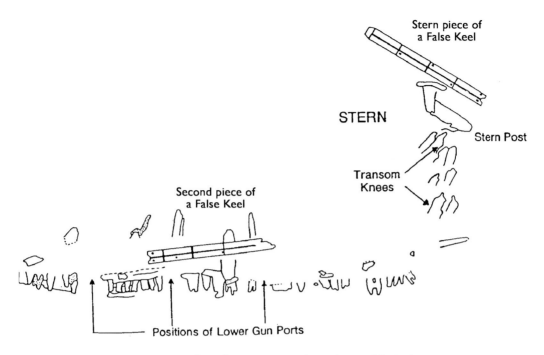

Figure 80. Extract from the 1985 survey shows the two false keel sections.

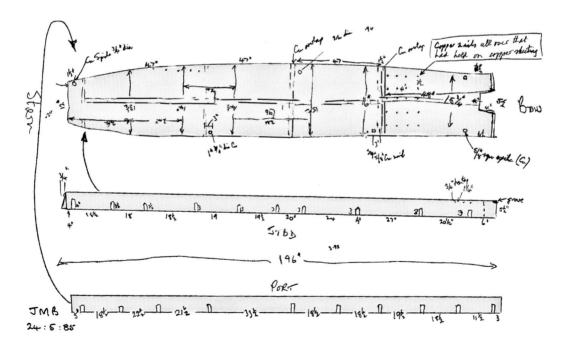

Figure 81. John Bingeman's rough sketch of the false keel stern section.

What is not clear is whether these false keel sections with a width of only 41cm (16in) could have belonged to *Invincible*. They might have come from a later grounding by another ship at the wreck site. *Invincible*'s keel measurements were not recorded in the 1747 Survey[2] but the width of the keelson was given as 64 cm (25in), much wider than the 41cm of these sections. One would have expected the keelson, keel and false keel to have similar dimensions. While one cannot be certain, it seems unlikely that the two stern located false keel sections belonged to *Invincible*.

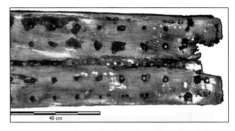

Figure 82. The right hand end of the false keel drawing Fig. 81. Photograph John Bingeman.

Figure 80 shows these two false keel sections lying on the seabed. The stern section was recovered and is illustrated in the Licensee's drawing (Fig. 81) and partly photographed (Fig. 82). The second section with the fractured end was measured and drawn by the Licensee while underwater and is in his diving report dated 16th June 1985. Its overall length was 4.13m and the damaged end appears in the isometric drawing of the small investigative trench dug in 1985 (Fig. 53). This section was unfortunately lost during gales, having been partly exposed by the 1985 investigative trench.

False keel bow section

A rather different copper nailed false keel section (Fig. 83) with a broken off length of 1.22m was recovered near *Invincible*'s bow. Its location near the bow and the use of copper nails, pre-dating copper sheathing, seems more likely than the stern sections to have belonged to *Invincible*. Even before copper nail studding, large headed iron nails were used for the same purpose as an early method of protection against teredo worms. The substitution of copper nails seems to have reflected an appreciation of the poisonous effect of that metal on living organisms. Full copper sheathing was introduced some twenty years later following the successful *Alarm* trial in 1760. The Author's paper on that subject provides more details.[3]

To secure a false keel

The false keel sections were secured on either side of the main keel by regular spaced copper staples, a method that allowed them to be readily replaced if damaged. The regular staple 'slots' can be seen on Figure 81 and a single 'slot' on Figure 83. The sixteen staples recovered varied in condition from good with both 'spikes' to severely eroded with only one 'spike'. Their spans varied from 210 to 245mm in length, their bodies were common at 10 × 30mm with 'spike' lengths of 110mm.

An occasional copper nail (Fig. 85) was found driven home through the false keel's underside straight into the main keel; these were probably there to hold the keel in position while the staples were fitted. It had a square profile of 17 × 14mm and if the shank had not eroded away would have measured 203 to 229mm (8 to 9 in).

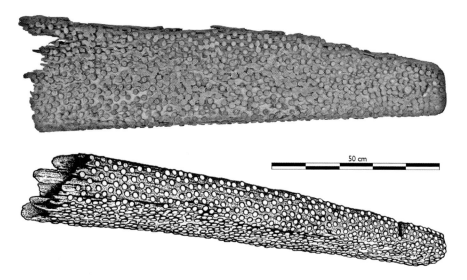

Figure 83. Top: false keel vertical view, photograph Geoff Lee. Bottom: drawing by Norman C. Lacey. Length 1.22 metres, Inv/80/021.

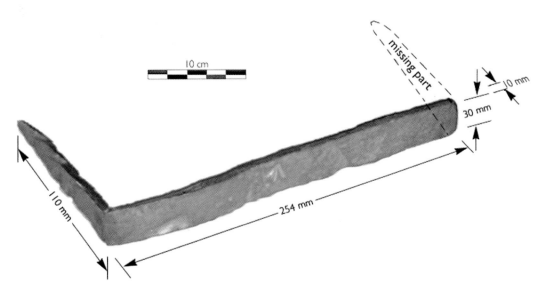

Figure 84. A typical copper staple. Photograph John P. Bethell.

Figure 85. False keel copper nail with broad arrow just visible. Photograph John Bingeman.

Wooden flange pieces

Four of these elm flange pieces were recovered and their purpose remains a mystery. All four had been in service and each had corroded remains of two securing ferrous nails. The illustrated flange Inv/86/057 had been handmade, while its twins had been lathe turned and were slightly smaller at 122mm diameter after stabilization.

Iron knees

Traditionally, oak was used for all hanging, rising (also called 'standard') and lodging knees used in shipbuilding to reinforce the strength of a ship's hull. British shipbuilders had started to use wrought iron knees as early as 1706 but they were not used

Figure 86. Elm flange piece, outside diameter 134mm before and 125mm after conservation, Inv/86/057. Photograph John Bingeman.

extensively.[4] It was the French, perhaps driven by a shortage of suitably shaped wooden timber, who took up their use enthusiastically. In the 1747 Survey Report of *Invincible*, it records the use of over 200 iron knees.[5]

A number of these iron knees used within *Invincible*'s hull were seen during excavations and two were brought to the surface.

Figure 87 is the Licensee's isometric underwater sketch of an iron hanging knee supporting the deck beam 'LG-5' after the pine wood panelling had been removed. The knee was partly countersunk into an oak pad piece. A screw nut can be seen at the knee's bottom arm, presumably for tightening during service. The sketch also shows the overlapping panelling that covered the ship's inner hull planking. Figure 88 shows the same knee 'LG-5' (5th deck beam on Gun Deck port side) redrawn to scale by a Naval Wren Illustrator.

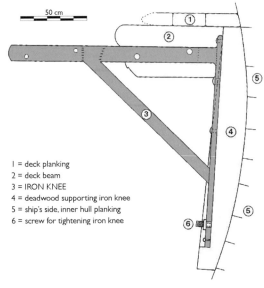

1 = deck planking
2 = deck beam
3 = IRON KNEE
4 = deadwood supporting iron knee
5 = ship's side, inner hull planking
6 = screw for tightening iron knee

Figure 87. Plan of hanging knee 'LG-5'.

Pieces of wrought iron were joined together by hammer welding after heating to a 'cherry red' temperature. In Figure 90 the iron knee triangular strengthening block is shown. The effects of hammer welding are addressed in the following paragraph.

A study of the second iron knee (Inv/87/103) was the subject of a set of studies made by a student at Portsmouth Polytechnic. These comprised (a) the method of production; (b) Knoop hardness tests; (c) the effect of seawater corrosion on the wrought iron; (d) the identification of slag inclusions (including micrographs); (e) the difference in grain sizes between the area of hammer welds and the rest of the knee; (f) the extra hardness caused by hammer welding. His results are published in his thesis.[6]

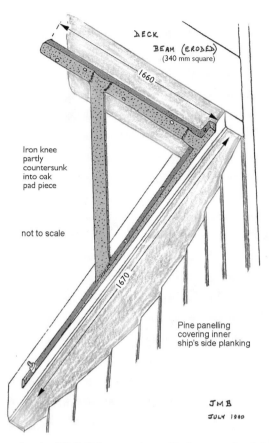

Figure 88. Isometric sketch of 'LG-5' hanging knee. Underwater sketch by John Bingeman.

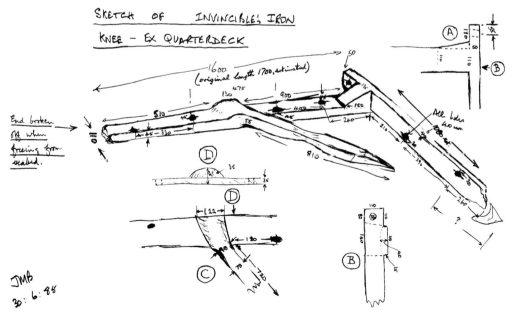

Figure 89. Sketch of the iron knee, Inv/85/042. Drawing John Bingeman.

Figure 90. Hanging knee before and after cleaning, Inv/85/042. Photographs John Bingeman.

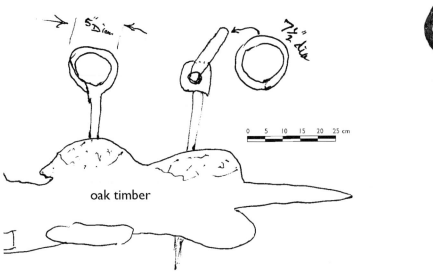

Figure 91. Right-hand end of oak timber with two iron fittings. John Bingeman's diving log drawing dated 13th October 1986.

Figure 92. The right-hand wrought iron fitting from Fig. 91 with attachment ring. Diameter 190mm, Inv/86/359. Photograph John Bingeman.

Iron bulwark fittings

A detached piece of oak timber 2.3 metres long had two iron fittings as illustrated in Figure 91. It is likely to have been part of *Invincible*'s bulwarks. It was partly submerged lying 3.5 metres to the west of LG-5 iron knee. The right-hand fitting had a ring diameter 7½ inches (190mm); the left hand fitting had an eye diameter 5 inches (137mm).

Figure 93. Elm octagonal pump tube. Length 1050mm, Inv/86/336. Photograph Peter Hales.

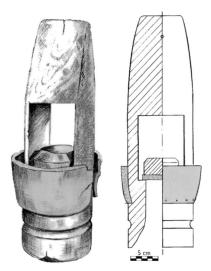

Figure 94. Hand pump non-return valve elm and leather, Inv/84/360. Drawing/ sketch John R. Terry.

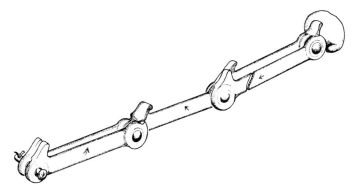

Figure 95. Drawing by John R. Terry.

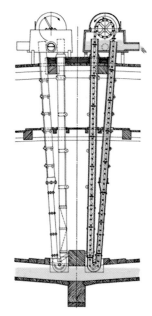

Figure 96. Pomone's chain pump sealing disc. Diameter 6½ inches (165mm), thickness 3mm.

Figure 97. Victory's chain pump in operation based on John McKay's drawing.[8]

Pumps

Non-return valves (Fig. 94) would be placed inside the elm pump tube illustrated in Figure 93. The elm tube had the same internal diameter to match the outside diameter of both the recovered non-return valves. The valve which is not illustrated (Inv/81/212) measured 338mm in height.

Chain pumps

It is known from the Court Martial transcript[7] referred to in Chapter 1 that *Invincible* was fitted with four chain pumps, but no artefacts from these pumps were recovered. The Licensee had previously recovered three links from *Pomone's* (1805–11) chain pump. The bronze chain links are designed with 'hooks' to engage the operating drum as shown in Figure 95.

The chain links had regularly placed brass sealing discs to hold a leather 'cup' shaped washer – see Figure 96. The disc had eight 10mm spikes to retain the leather washer.

In Figure 96, a 'cup' shaped leather seal would increase the diameter to 7 inches. Material is actually brass but looks like copper due to dezincification.

Invincible and *Pomone's* chain pumps would have been very similar in design to *Victory's* pumps except they would have had slightly shorter suction tubes. The tube diameter in *Pomone* was 7 inches. The sealing 'discs' in *Victory* were fitted to every sixth link.

Rigging

Rigging blocks

The majority of the blocks came from the Boatswain and Gunner's separate store rooms on the port side of the Orlop deck.

The Boatswain's Store was an 'Aladdin's cave' containing a whole range of different types of spare blocks including replacement sheaves and pins. Perhaps the most unusual were a 58 inch rack block and a 28 inch euphroe block. The largest of the spare lignum vitae pins measured 21 inches by 3 inches diameter (Fig. 98) indicating that there must have been a double or treble block even larger than those recovered.

In the Gunner's Store among the various other contents, there were both single and double 10 inch blocks used for working the gun carriage tackles.

Figure 98. Spare lignum vitae pin. Length 21in. × 3in. diameter, Inv/81/180.

Figure 99. Artefacts exposed in the Gunner's Store before recovery. Photograph John Broomhead.

Figure 100. Ten single sheaved blocks sized from 5 to 21 inches. Photograph by Peter Hales.

Single blocks

A complete range of types and sizes of single blocks, from the 5 to 21 inches (Fig. 100), to four large topsail halyard 'flat' blocks (Fig. 104) were removed. The majority had their sizes marked on their respective shells using Arabic numerals up to 9 inches, and then Roman numerals for the larger sizes. These sizes referred to the maximum dimension of the oval shaped shells. Also, most blocks were marked with at least one broad arrow.

The majority of blocks over 9 inches had conventional Roman numerals. The following were the exceptions:

> 12in. had 'J2'
> 18in. had 'J8'
> 21in. had '2J'

(A 'J' representing a '1' – a common 18th Century practice)

Block shrinkage

In 2008, Figure 101 had a 20¾ inch shell with a 3¼ inch wide sheave. The width of this extra-strong single block, known as a 'clump block', was 11 inches, and the lignum vitae pin had a length of 11¾ inches by 2½ inch diameter. The fact that the pin measured 11¾ inches vis-à-vis the present block thickness of 11 inches shows the shell had contracted by three quarters of an inch during conservation and the 22 intervening years. The lignum vitae measurements remain constant while the elm has shrunk.

Wear and tear to pins

The Boatswain's store was crammed with spares, from complete blocks of all types to lignum vitae wheels and pins of different sizes. Besides these, there were severely worn pins; three are illustrated in Figures 102 and 103 to show wear during service.

Topsail halyard blocks

A total of four topsail halyard blocks were recovered, two of these are illustrated Figure 104. The block sheaves were rather thinner than one would have expected for such large blocks; their respective thicknesses were: 1¾in for the 24in and only 1½in for the 25 and 28 inch blocks. Their shells were elm and the sheaves and pins were lignum vitae.

Figure 101. 21 in. (2J) single block, Inv/86/229. Photograph Geoff Lee taken in 2008.

Figure 102. Left: 6 × 1¾in diameter. Right: 3¾ × 1in diameter. Large: Inv/87/013 Small: Inv/NK. Photograph John Bingeman.

Figure 103. Example of wear on a double block, Inv/86/176. Photograph John Bingeman.

Figure 104. Topsail halyard 28 and 24 inch blocks. Photograph Peter Hales.

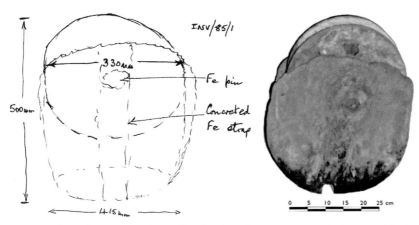

Figure 105. Drawing from the Licensee's diving log dated 28th May 1985; and photograph before conservation.

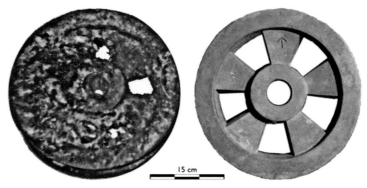

Figure 106. Before and after conservation, the 13 inch (330mm) bronze sheave with broad arrow, Inv/85/001.

List of topsail halyard blocks

24in.   Inv/86/070 and 139
         – marked 'XXIIII'
25in.   Inv/86/028 – marked
         'XXV'
28in.   Inv/86/078 – marked
         'XXVIII'

Snatch blocks

Two snatch blocks were recovered during the eleven years of excavations. The largest (Fig. 105) was particularly

Figure 107. The 11½ inch (329mm) snatch block, Inv/87/048. From: Heart of Oak – A Sailors Life in Nelson's Navy *by James P. McGuane. © 2002 James P. McGuane. Used by permission of W. W. Norton and Company.*

interesting as it had a 13 inch bronze sheave with a broad arrow. Its elm shell, the ferrous strap and pin were severely degraded.

The second snatch block (Fig. 107) was rather more conventional with an elm shell and lignum vitae pin and sheave. It was found in the smaller cooking cauldron (Fig. 304) where the block's ferrous catch had corroded away.

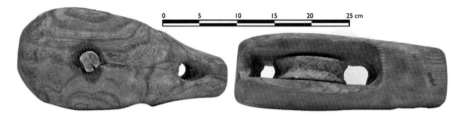

Figure 108. Medieval-style block. Length 278, width 128, and depth 85mm. Sheave diameter 95 x 26mm, Inv/86/041. Photographs Geoff Lee.

Medieval-style block

Figure 108 shows the one exception to the hundreds of rigging blocks from *Invincible* that all had sheaves and pins of lignum vitae. Lignum vitae is an extremely hard, oily wood from the Caribbean that came into use during the 17th century. This block appears to belong to an earlier, even medieval, period with an elm shell and what is thought to be an ash sheave and pin. When recovered, it had a short length of rope through its eye.

Summary of the single blocks recovered

List of 'standard' blocks

5in.	Inv/80/069 and 89/138
6in.	Inv/81/004 and 81/006
6½in.	84/177, 86/239, 87/018 and 019, and 88/060
7in.	Inv/83/082
8in.	Inv/80/208 and 223, 84/248, 86/218, 277 and 313, 87/035 and 248, 88/283
9in.	Inv/81/176 and 88/024
10in.	Inv/79/014, 80/144, 207, 211 and 279, 83/236, 84/001, 072, 247, 292, 293, 307, 372 and 373, 88/084
11in.	Inv/84/002 and 86/003
12in.	Inv/80/181(J2), 84/308, 86/233(XII), 341(XII) and 88/085(XII)
14in.	Inv/83/009(XIIII) and 050, 86/001(XIIII) and 002(XIIII), 86/069, 86/(all with XIIIIs) 091, 189, 230, 232 and 357, 87/003(XIIII), 004 and 88/007
15in.	Inv/84/201, and 86/043(XV).
16in.	Inv/84/015(XVI), 090, 118 and 355, and 88/031(with 'XVI')
17in.	Inv/86/188(XVII and double strop grooves), 84/137(XVII)
18in.	Inv/86/016, 231(XVIII) and 277(XVIII), 85/064(XVIII), and 88/086(J8).
20in.	Inv/84/027(XX), 86/068(XX), and 86/185(XX with double strop grooves).
21in.	Inv/86/229("2J" and double strop grooves).

Topsail halyard 'flat' blocks

24in.	Inv/86/070 stamped 'XXIIII'
25in.	Inv/86/028 stamped 'XXV'
28in.	Inv/86/078 and Inv/87/136 stamped 'XXVIII'

Snatch blocks

Inv/85/001 Size not known, the recovered half shell measured 335mm holding a bronze sheave diameter 330mm.

Inv/87/048 Length 329mm.

Double blocks

The largest number of double blocks were in the Gunner's Store; these were all 10 inch and would have been spares for gun carriage tackles.

In the Boatswain's Store, double block sizes ranged from 8 inches up to a massive 27 inch. A slightly smaller 26½ inch block Figure 109 had a 'TB' label attached and was probably 27 inches before conservation, the same size as the largest 27 inch double block (Inv/84/135).

What 'TB' stood for is uncertain. 'Top Block' seems the most obvious and I have found the term used for 'swaying' (hoisting) topmasts.[9] However, the only reference and illustration of a 'top block' is a single block, iron bound with hook and appears to be 19th century in style. The massive double block kept in the Boatswain's Store may indeed have been a 'Top Block'.

List of double blocks

8in.	Inv/87/147
10in.	Inv/80/002, 143, 180, 202, 210 and 221, 83/096, 84/244, 260, 261, 273, 294, 303, 315 and 328
13in.	Inv/86/144 and 354
14in.	Inv/86/238
15in.	Inv/86/237
26½in.	Inv/86/110
27in.	Inv/84/135

Treble blocks

Figure 111 shows an impressive 20 inch treble block with elm shell and lignum vitae sheaves and pin. A similar second block was recovered (Inv/86/338).

Figure 109. Double block with 'TB' wooden label, Inv/86/110. Elm shell and lignum vitae pin and sheaves. Photograph Peter Hales.

Figure 110. The enlarged 'TB' elm label – the same carving is repeated on the reverse, and a 'union flag' is carved on the square end on the left of the 'T', Inv/86/110.

Figure 111. Twenty inch treble block, Inv/86/080. Elm shell and lignum vitae pin and sheaves. Photograph Peter Hales.

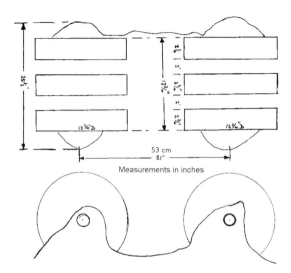

Figure 112. John Bingeman's underwater sketch of eroded tandem treble block – plan and side views. Report dated 26th May 1985.

Figure 113. One of the six treble-block lignum vitae 12¾ inch sheaves with bronze coak held by iron rivets, Inv/85/081. Photograph Peter Hales (top), John Bingeman (bottom 2).

Tandem treble block

Lying close to the surface to the east of the main site bow area were two large iron-reinforced treble blocks (Inv/85/081). They lay joined together in tandem with 21 inch between pin sheave centres, within a badly eroded common structure, width 25½ inch (original structure length not clear due to erosion) – see Figure 112 sketch. The six lignum vitae sheaves were 12¾ inches in diameter with

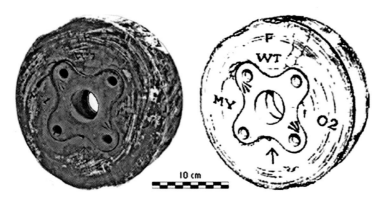

Figure 114. Pomone's 8 inch sheave with bronze coaks fitted either side. 'WT' = Walter Taylor, 'MY' = May, '02' = 1802. Photograph Peter Hales, drawing John R. Terry.

Figure 115. A bronze coak ex-Pomone (1811). The centre hole showed considerable signs of wear. Photograph John Bingeman.

bronze square-shaped coaks marked with a broad arrow. These coaks are rather different in design from those found on Walter Taylor blocks manufactured later in the 18th century.

Whether the double treble-block structure had been part of the catting head or a structure at the base of a mast is not known. It might even have been brought out to the site during the attempted salvage operation to save *Invincible*.

In Figure 113, the top photograph was taken in 1985. The 2007 photographs shows slight deterioration probably attributable to the corrosion of one of the iron rivets.

Development of block sheaves

Wear to lignum vitae pins under constant use is severe, and they need replacing frequently. The firm of Walter Taylor in Bugle Street, Southampton had the contract to supply the Admiralty with blocks and at the height of this contract they were supplying up to 100,000 blocks a year. A third-rate alone was reputed to need 1,500 blocks. Figure 114 is an eight inch Taylor block fitted with a pair of bronze coaks, and was recovered from the *Pomone* wreck site. These bronze coaks were manufactured in two halves and secured together by four ferrous rivets. This is a development from the *Invincible* 12¾ inch sheave (Fig. 113) with a coak in one piece and attached on one side only with two rivets.

The firm of Walter Taylor lost trade when Marc Isambard Brunel designed his block making machines. Brunel, father of the even more famous Isambard Kingdom Brunel offered his machines to Samuel Taylor, Walter's son, who declined the offer. Brunel then went to the Admiralty and set up the famous block mills at Portsmouth Dockyard in 1803. Two years later, Walter Taylor's firm lost their lucrative Admiralty contract.

The coaks in smaller sized sheaves had three 'arms' rather than four. The Figure 115 example was recovered without any trace of its lignum vitae wheel; its actual sheave size was unknown.

Fiddle blocks

The purpose of fiddle blocks was to control main sails when double blocks would affect the air flow. Figure 116 illustrates one of the eight sizes of fiddle blocks that ranged from 24 to 34 inches with intermediate sizes of 27, 28, 29, 30, 32 and 33 inches. The two largest had lignum vitae sheave diameters of 9 and 15 inches – see side view in Figure 117.

List of fiddle blocks

24in.	Inv/84/136
27in.	(size uncertain but thought to be 27 inch) Inv/88/015
28in.	Inv/81/121 and 301, Inv/84/130, Inv/85/080 (with XXVIII), and Inv/86/187 and 356
29in.	Inv/86/081 (with XXVIIII)
30in.	Inv/86/140 (with broad arrow)
32in.	Inv/86/014 (with XXXII)
33in.	Inv/86/026
34in.	Inv/80/307 and Inv/84/026

Total: 14 fiddle blocks

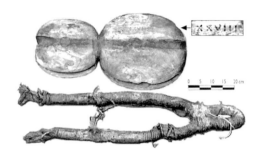

Figure 116. A 'XXVIII' (28 inch) fiddle block with rope strop, Inv/85/080. Photograph Peter Hales.

Deadeyes

Deadeyes (Fig. 118) were used with standing rigging to create a purchase when tensioning shrouds. A number of deadeyes had traces of metal bands in various states of corrosion; these are bracketed in the following list with the word 'iron'.

Sizes ranged from 3½ to 18 inch diameter and had similar size markings to rigging blocks; namely, those up to 9 inches had Arabic numerals, and those of 10 inches and above had Roman numerals. Some had broad arrows; they were all made from elm except for one 8 inch deadeye made of beech.

Figure 117. Thirty-four inch fiddle block, Inv/80/307. Photograph Peter Hales.

Figure 118. Six elm deadeyes from 5 to 14 inches diameter. Photograph Peter Hales.

List of deadeyes

3½in.   Inv/86/366 – size unmarked, no broad arrow
5in.   Inv/80/124
6in.   Inv/86/027 – incorrectly marked 7″
7in.   Inv/80/142, 84/013, 86/055, 251, 252, 267 and 342, 87/026, 097 and 114, and 88/009
8in.   Inv/84/134 (different style in beech), 87/094 (iron) and 87/115
9in.   Inv/80/219, 86/142 and 197 (both with broad arrows), and 87/225
10in.   Inv/86/141, 196 and 250, and 87/109 (with "X")
11in.   Inv/81/207, 83/213, 84/023 (iron), 86/039 and 044, and 87/204
12in.   Inv/81/062, 84/066, 86/195 and 249 (both with broad arrows), 87/107 (iron), and 87/108 ('X11' and iron)
14in.   Inv/86/013
16in.   Inv/88/290
18in.   Inv/81/122 and Inv/87/025 (XVIII)

Heart blocks

Heart blocks (Fig. 119) were used in standing rigging in a similar way to deadeyes. The three depicted from left to right are:

    14 inch plain style marked 'XIIII' Inv/86/340
    12 inch with a triangular hole (Inv/86/253)
    13 inch with four rope grooves at the base of the 'triangle' (Inv/86/038).
    A fourth 8 inch heart block was also recovered (Inv/80/177).

'Bull's-eye' cringle

Elm 'bull's-eye' cringles were used at the tack (corner) of a sail – see Figures 120, 121 and 122.

Six much larger 8 inch elm cringles (Fig. 123) were found together in good condition, all but one had a broad arrow (Inv/84/017, 018, 019, 020, 021 (without broad arrow), and 84/022).

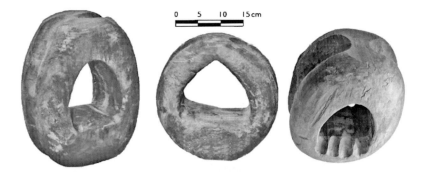

Figure 119. Three designs of elm heart blocks. Photographs Peter Hales (left two), Geoff Lee (right).

Figure 120. Elm 'bull's-eye' cringle used at the tack (corner) of a sail. Diameter 2¾ inches, Inv/87/079 or 117 (both identical). Photographs John Bingeman.

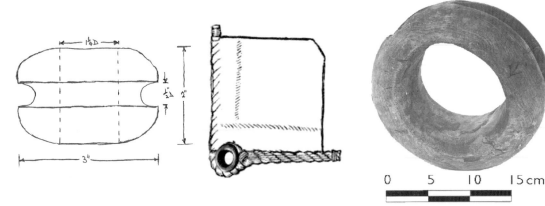

Figures 121 and 122. John Bingeman's diving log drawing dated 20th May 1987 of a 3 inch 'bull's-eye' cringle, Inv/87/007 with an illustration showing its use. Drawing John P. Bethell.

Figure 123. Eight inch elm cringle with broad arrow, Inv/84/022. Photograph J. A. Hewes.

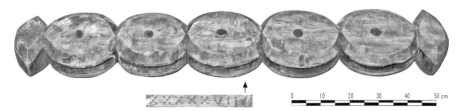

Figure 124. A 'XXXXXVIII' Rack block – a solid elm shell houses five single blocks, Inv/86/042 Photograph Peter Hales.

Rack block

The unusual 58 inch rack block (Fig. 124) would have been used as one of a pair lashed either side of the bowsprit. Its purpose is to provide leads for sheets (operating ropes) for the spritsail(s) beneath the bowsprit – see Figure 126. Also recovered was a single 10 inch block that had been a broken end from a 58 inch rack block (Fig. 125). There was also a single 10 inch block (Inv/88/115) later identified as the centre section of a rack block and stamped '..XXXVIII'.

Figure 125. The broken-off end of a rack block, Inv/84/142. These rack blocks are simply five 10 inch blocks in a single elm shell. Photograph John Bingeman.

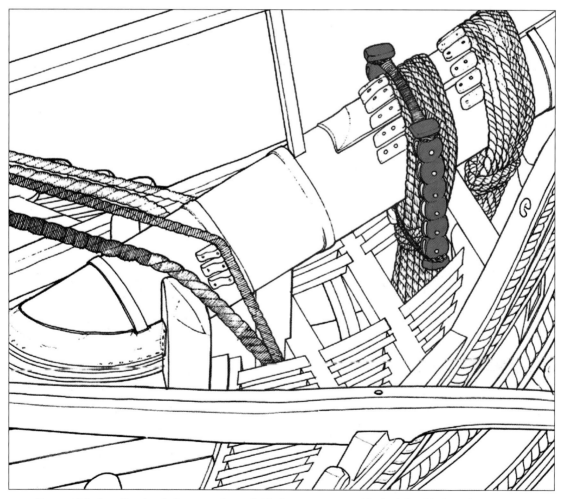

Figure 126. Jean Boudriot's drawing of a rack block in situ. Invincible *had five blocks rather than six.*[10]

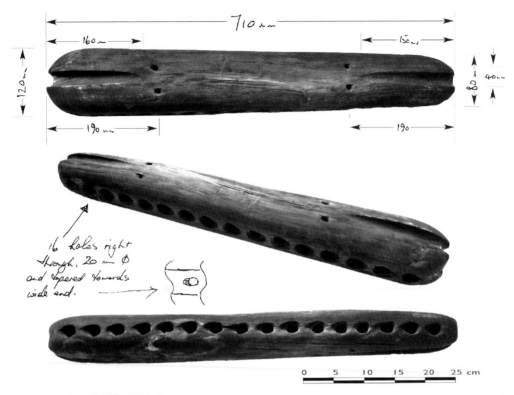

Figure 127. John Broomhead's measurements from his Diving Report dated 19/5/86, Inv/86/017. Photographs Geoff Lee.

Euphroe block

The single elm euphroe or euvro block (Fig. 127) had a length of 710mm (28in) tapered from 120 to 80mm. To secure a strop, it was grooved at either end and augmented by two pairs of small holes for a whipping. At right angles to the line of the strop, there are sixteen equally spaced 20mm diameter holes tapered towards the wider end. The purpose of the euphroe block was to be a centre point so that light ropes could be secured in a fan shape to suspend an awning. The arrangement is known as a crowfoot.

Clew-garnet blocks

Clew-garnet blocks (Figs 128 and 129) were used with tackles to furl sails quickly by hoisting them upwards and inwards. The name came from their attachment to the lower corners of a square sail known as a 'clew'; the 'garnet' part is more obscure but may be its resemblance to a pomegranate. The French for pomegranate was 'grenat'; and this word was also used in medieval English becoming 'garnet'.

Like other blocks, clew-garnet shells were made from elm and their pin and sheave from lignum vitae.

The 15 inch clew block shown on the right hand of Figure 128 is a different design with a 'mushroom' head. Although it stands 15 inches high, it is marked "XVI" (16 inch). It is unknown whether this was intentional or an error. It is also stamped with a broad arrow.

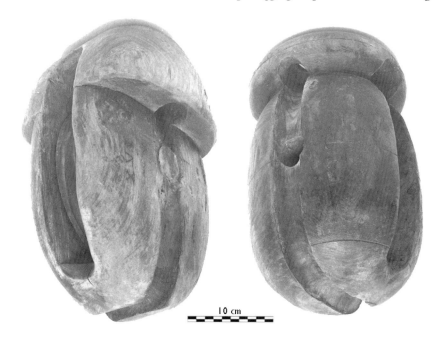

Figure 128. Left is the 'standard' clew block Inv/86/037, right is a variation, Inv/86/040. Photographs J. A. Hewes.

List of clew blocks

11in.	Inv/86/003 stamped 'XI'
	14in. Inv/86/234 stamped 'XIIII'
15in.	Inv/86/040 different style, see note below
	16in. Inv/86/037, 088* and 235 stamped 'XVI', and 86/023 stamped 'J6'.
17in.	Inv/86/190

Shroud trucks

A total of 95 shroud trucks were recovered. In the Boatswain's Store thirty were in a bag that disintegrated during recovery. These trucks were bound to standing rigging to provide a lead or guide for running ropes that passed through their centres. They came in two sizes, see Figure 130.

Parrel trucks and ribs

Parrel trucks (balls) with spacer ribs, both made of elm, were used to secure the centre of a yard to a mast. This arrangement allows the yard to move up and down and to turn on the mast as required, see Figure 134. The rib sizes were: 12, 14, 18, 20, 22, 27, 28, 30 and 36 inches in length (Figs 131 132 and 133). The 30 and 36 inch sizes were designed for three bands of trucks – see Figure 133. Most of the ribs had at least one broad arrow. The trucks recovered had diameters of: 2¾, 3, 3½, 5 and 6 inches; two of the 5 inch trucks had a single broad arrow.

*Inv/86/088 had the 'V' of the 'XVI' inverted.

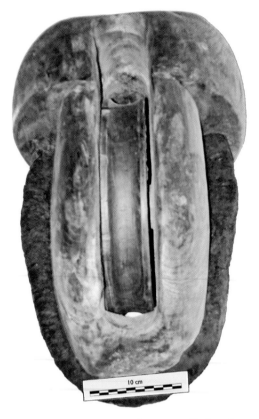

Figure 130. Two sizes of shroud trucks. Left: 4 × 3 inch diameter, Inv/84/457. Right: 3¾ × 3¼ inch diameter, Inv/NK.

Figure 129. Seventeen inch clew-garnet block with rope strop "circle" still attached, Inv/86/190. Photograph John Bingeman.

Figure 131. A pair of 12-inch parrel ribs with 3½-inch trucks held by a length of Invincible's rope. Photograph John Bingeman.

Figure 132. A 12 inch elm parrel rib – 'XII' can just be seen on the left side. It also has a broad arrow, Inv/81/153. Photograph John Bingeman.

Figure 133. A 36 inch elm parrel rib, hole diameters 2¼ inch – there are two small holes (one visible) for assembly purposes, Inv/88/228. Photograph John Bingeman.

Ropes and Cables

Ropes recovered range in sizes from 1 inch to 23 inches circumference – see examples in Figure 135. The majority were hawser-laid rope. Rope was always measured by its circumference contrary to modern man-made fibre ropes which are measured by their diameter.

The ropes used for supporting the mast were known as 'standing rigging' while ropes used for controlling the sails were known as 'running rigging'.

Summary of rope sizes recovered
Hawser-laid: 1, 1¼, 1½, 2½, 3, 3½, 4½, 6, and 23 inches.
A complete coil of one inch – see Figure 136.
Cable-laid: 9 and 14 inches – see Figure 137.

Lightly tarred 9 and 14 inch cable-laid rope were found in large flat coils on the Orlop deck ready for use, see Figure 138.

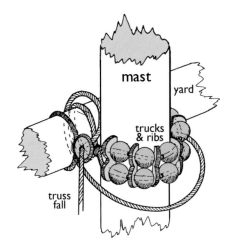

Figure 134. Illustration to show the use of parrel trucks and ribs. Drawing John P. Bethell.

Excavation of the 23-inch hawser cable was very difficult as it disintegrated when touched. A technique was developed to stop the disintegration by delicately binding the rope with thin medical bandages. By drying the ropes very slowly, their structural strength returned, and the bandages could be safely removed. Two short lengths were successfully recovered (Fig. 139).

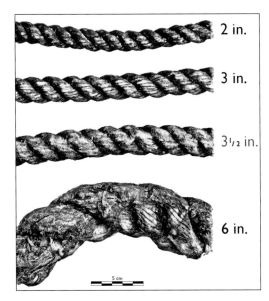

Figure 135. Examples of 'hawser or plain-laid' ropes. Photograph John Bingeman.

Figure 136. A complete coil of 1 inch rope, Inv/83/151. Photograph John Bingeman.

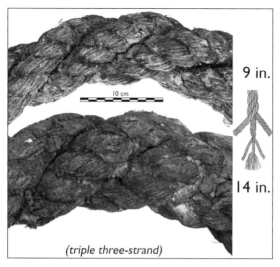

Figure 137. Sections of 9 and 14 inch cable-laid rope recovered from the Orlop deck. The illustration on the right shows the structure of cable-laid rope. Photograph John Bingeman.

Figure 138. The Licensee recording details of a coil of 9 inch cable-laid rope on the Orlop deck. Photograph Christopher Dobbs.

Figure 139. Two lengths of the 23-inch hawser cable under conservation, Inv/88/294 and 88/309.

Hawser tube

The hawser tube (Fig. 140) was the heaviest artefact lifted. It was lying on the seabed close to the bow. The 23-inch hawser cable would have passed through the tube. On both flange ends there were regular small holes to secure the tube to the hull as seen in Figure 141.[11]

Figure 140. Lead hawser tube, two views. Diameter 370mm, height 680mm, Inv/81/015. Photographs John Bingeman.

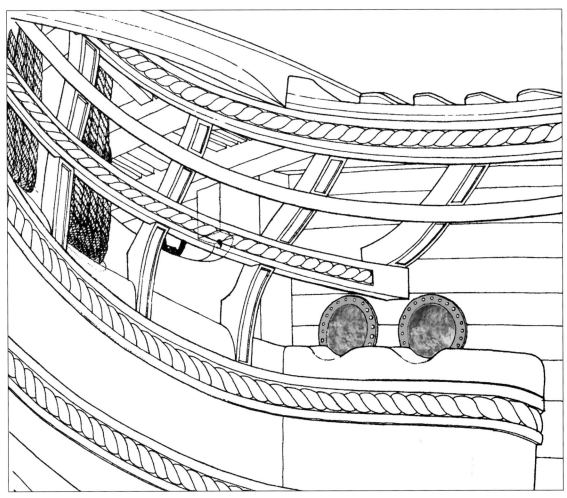

Figure 141. Jean Boudriot's drawing of hawser tubes.

Rope treatment

The standing rigging ropes would have been well dressed with Swedish tar. The pine barrel (Fig. 142) was recovered close to the Ship's Boatswain's store and is thought to have been in use at the time of the wrecking. Some of the barrel staves had been snapped off to make easier access to the bottom of the drum. Underwater, the tar was no longer solid and the two divers responsible for the barrel's recovery became liberally coated in tar! White spirit removed it.

Figure 142. Tar barrel, height as seen 660mm, Inv/86/071. Photograph John Bingeman.

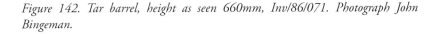

Serving mallets

The two serving mallets in Figures 143 and 144 were used by the Bosun's Party to 'serve' ropes to protect them from excessive wear – see Figure 145.

The term 'parcelling' (Fig. 145) will be referred to again in Chapter 6 when leather used for rope protection is discussed.

Fids

Several sizes of fid were recovered from the smallest at 85mm (Fig. 146) to the largest at 735mm known as an 'Admiral'. Other small fids of various shapes and sizes are illustrated in Figure 149.

Figure 147 is a regular size for splicing ropes; the type of hardwood was never identified. While the artefact was classified as a fid, it was suggested that it could be a belaying pin. Personally, I consider

Figure 143. Serving mallet with groove at the top. Head measurement 8 × 4 inches diameter, Inv/80/117. From: Heart of Oak – A Sailors Life in Nelson's Navy *by James P. McGuane.© 2002 James P. McGuane. Used by permission of W. W. Norton and Company.*

Figure 144. Serving mallet with side 'groove'. Head measurements 7 × 3 inches diameter, Inv/80/131. Photograph Peter Hales.

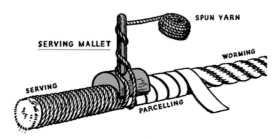

Figure 145. Illustration to show how a serving mallet is used. Admiralty Manual of Seamanship.[12]

this to be incorrect as it was significantly different from a number of slightly thinner and differently styled belaying pins made of oak; none of the oak belaying pins had broad arrows.

The 'Admiral' fid was made of yew (Fig. 148); it measured 735mm in length, diameter 145mm. Originally it would have measured 30 inches (763mm) with a diameter of 6 inches (152mm). Its likely use would have been to splice *Invincible*'s 23-inch anchor hawser cable.

Figure 146. A delightful 85mm fid in mint condition – unidentified hardwood – Inv/90/019. Photograph John Bingeman.

Figure 147. A hardwood fid 412mm long with a pair of broad arrows, Inv/80/109. Photograph Peter Hales.

Figure 148. The 'Admiral' fid, Inv/80/119. Photograph Geoffrey Lee.

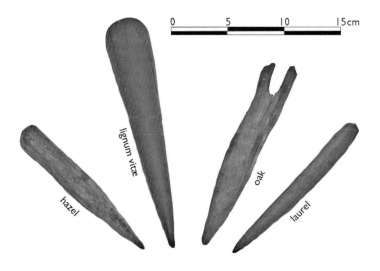

Figure 149. Other small fids of various shapes and sizes. Lengths (left to right): 152, 229, 197 and 152mm. Reference (left to right) Inv/s: 84/443, 86/200, 84/112 and 86/149. Centre left 229mm was made of lignum vitae, Inv/86/200. Centre right in oak, 197mm long, Inv/84/112. Two outer both 152mm long: in elm, Inv/84/443 and laurel, Inv/86/149.

Navigation

Compass

After *Invincible's* grounding, stores were apparently collected in the forward half of the ship ready to be landed. Two cooking cauldrons were found full of various artefacts ready to be hoisted out; they were for some reason abandoned. Adjacent to these cauldrons, perhaps ready for a subsequent load, was a compass (Fig. 150) in a gimballed box and close by were sounding leads. Various parts of sand glasses including glass bowl shards were among the debris in this area. Fortunately six sandglasses, two 30-minute, two 28-second and two 14-second glasses survived intact. Parts of a log line reel and a log-ship were recovered.

Pieces of broken glass (Fig. 153) were found within the compass bowl (Fig. 151); also, other semi-transparent pieces (Fig. 152) about 1mm thick were found. Their exact significance is not known but it

Figure 150. Compass bowl, Inv/87/135, with parts of the gimballed frame. The whole was contained in an oak box (Inv/87/150) with opening lid. Photograph Geoff Lee and John Bingeman.

Figure 151. View of inside the compass bowl with the central 'spike' to support the compass card, Inv/87/135. Photograph Geoff Lee.

Figure 152. Mica piece from compass, Inv/87/135. Photograph John Bingeman.

Figure 153. Broken glass from compass, Inv/87/135, 170 and 218. Photograph John Bingeman.

is surmised that they were part of the compass card. Following examination and tests the material was identified as mica that had been coated with shellac to minimise exfoliation. This study was carried out by Dr Brian Plunkett at Portsmouth Polytechnic.[13]

Only a single pair of navigation dividers was recovered during the eleven years of excavations (Fig. 154). Its ferrous points had corroded away.

Figure 154. Navigation dividers found within a concretion. Inv/84/314. Photograph John Bingeman.

Navigation 18-inch sector rule

The best description of *Invincible*'s multi-purpose rule (Fig. 155.1) could be: "a simple 18-inch folding rule with an astro-navigation sector capability. The two sector lines radiate out from the hinge pivot point where angles would be set using dividers. One of the two radial lines had 'γ' (Aries symbol) and 'P and S' that may stand for Polaris and the Sun. Two other letters 'MH' remain a mystery. Besides the logarithmic scales, there is a small regular spaced scale using even numbers at 11mm intervals from 28 to what would have been 14 if the brass hinge had not been broken off. It is assumed that

Rotated: Top = logarithmic scale from 1 to 10.
Side 1 = scales from 18 to 10 in. and 20 to 28 (?), log scale from 1.0 to 3.0.
Bottom with slot for c. 170 x 10 x 1.5 mm hinged metal arm.
Side 2 = log scales from 8 to 14 and from 15 to 30 plus number matrix.

Figure 155.1. Second half of a folding 'Navigation 18-inch sector rule', Inv/86/302. Photograph John Bingeman.

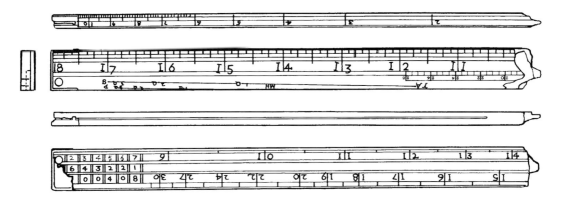

Figure 155.2. Scale: numbers 18 to 11 are in Imperial inches. Drawing John R. Terry.

'Arm B' would have had a similar scale from 14 to 0. This would suggest that it represented a lunar month and would be used as a scale to set dividers. It is possible that it was connected with the rule's '1Q', '2Q' and '3Q' representing the first, second and third quarters of the moon. On Side 2, there are two logarithmic scales and a numerical matrix whose purpose is not known.

It would be fascinating to know exactly how the rule was used. Research has revealed many similar styles starting with the Gunter rule from the 17th century. None are exactly similar to *Invincible's* rule, and there is no detailed information on how these rules were used.

Figure 155.3 illustrates a ferrous rectangular blade that would have been housed in the ruler's slot. Whether it was engraved with calibrations is not known; its hinge pin is still present within the remains of the brass end cap.

Sandglasses

During sea passages, the naval watch system divided the 24 hours of each day into six four-hour watches with half the ship's company on watch and the other half off duty. Each four-hour watch was marked every 30 minutes by ringing the ship's quarterdeck bell. After the first 30 minutes, one bell would be

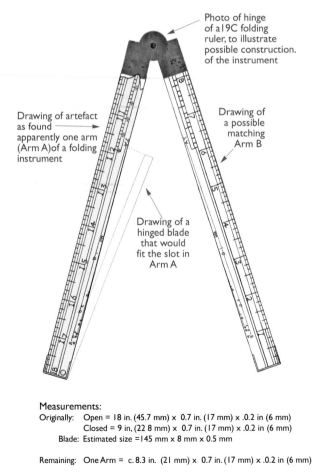

Measurements:
Originally: Open = 18 in. (45.7 mm) x 0.7 in. (17 mm) x .0.2 in (6 mm)
                    Closed = 9 in, (22 8 mm) x 0.7 in. (17 mm) x .0.2 in (6 mm)
    Blade: Estimated size =145 mm x 8 mm x 0.5 mm

Remaining: One Arm = c. 8.3 in. (21 mm) x 0.7 in. (17 mm) x .0.2 in (6 mm)

Figure 155.3. A reconstruction illustration by John P. Bethell.

sounded; thirty minutes later two bells, and so on up to eight bells at the end of the four-hour watch.

Like all ships of the period, *Invincible* used sandglasses to measure time. These were for two purposes: for watch-keeping and for estimating ships' speed. We found two sandglasses used for watch-keeping and four for estimating speed – see Figure 156. The two used for watch-keeping (Inv/79/013 and Inv/80/094) both measured the passage of 30 minutes (half-hour). A number of broken parts from longer duration sandglasses also used for watch-keeping are listed in the artefact record. The four for estimating speed measured an exact period when a marked log-line was run out over the stern, the number of knotted marks passing overboard providing a measure of the ship's speed in 'knots'. Two of each period were found: Inv/81/091 and Inv/83/075 of 28 seconds, called 'long', and Inv/84/096 and Inv/84/127 of 14 seconds, called 'short'. The 'short' glass (Figs 158 and 159) would have been used when *Invincible*'s speed exceeded 8 knots.

28 seconds   5 cm   30 minutes

Figure 156. A 28-second sandglass next to a 30-minute sandglass. Photograph Peter Hales.

5 cm

Figure 157. Half-hour sandglass, Inv/79/013, under conservation. At the centre bottom of the photograph is the partly eroded brass 'control disc' and only just visible is the very small regulating hole in its centre.

Figure 158. Sand pouring through the 14-second sandglass. Height 5 inches (127mm), Inv/84/096. Photograph John Bingeman.

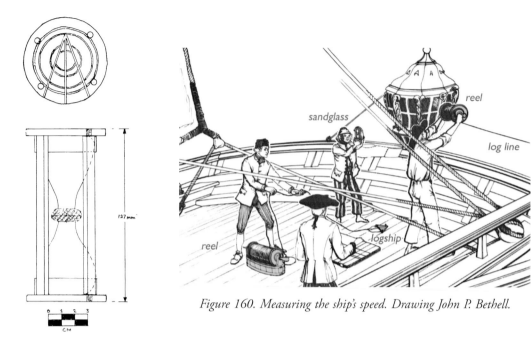

Figure 160. Measuring the ship's speed. Drawing John P. Bethell.

Figure 159. Licensee's drawing of the first of the two 14-second sandglasses recovered, Inv/84/096.

All sandglasses are of similar construction, although obviously of different physical size. The circular ends are all made of turned oak marked with a large broad arrow. The vertical posts are all pine, five on the 30-minute glasses but only four on the 28-second and 14-second glasses. The two 'bowls' are separated by a brass control disc with a small central hole and bound together with a sailmaker's whipping – see Figure 157.

The photograph in Figure 158 was taken with the sand pouring from top to bottom. The sandglass is all original except for the sailmaker's whipping in the centre.

So often, underwater visibility is negligible when all work is done by feel. The Licensee doesn't wear gloves since this is very delicate work. He wrote how it felt to find a sandglass in his diving report on the 5th June 1983:

'there were a number of fire wood blocks trapped under a shelf, and then I felt a circular disc that lifted off in my hand which had four spikes below; I knew I had found a 28 second 'hour' glass. I kept the air lift above the shelf and removed the mud gently away from the hourglass. After what seemed ages, I had gradually worked my way down to the bottom of the glass and was now feeling the bottom disc. I gently eased the whole hour glass minus the top from under the shelf to see it for the first time. It was just like finding my first 'Piece of Eight' (five years before at the Needles Wreck Site). My original diagnosis had been right, it was a '28 Second Hour Glass' used for measuring ship's speed knowing that the next size up has 5 legs and not four. I took it straight to the surface and placed it in a large sieve lowered over the side of the diving tender *Ceres*.' (This tender was the predecessor of my larger boat *Viney Peglar*.)

(The recovery refers to sandglass 'Inv/83/075')

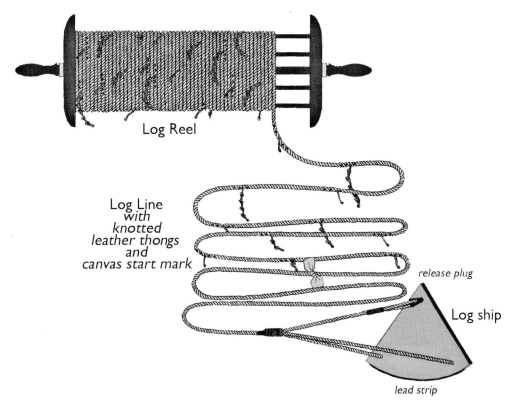

Log Reel

Log Line
with
knotted
leather thongs
and
canvas start mark

release plug

Log ship

lead strip

Figure 161. A typical log line.[14]

Log-ship

When recovered, the log-ship (Inv/87/086) was minus its lead weight which was found six weeks later. Prior to this a similar weight had been found but the nail holes did not match the wooden part of the log-ship. So it was a great relief when the second lead strip (Inv/87/128) holes matched the holes on the oak log-ship.

Since this log-ship was a spare (Fig. 162), the third and only tapered hole at the top had yet to be made. A wooden tapered plug on the third leg of the log line would have had to match the third hole on the log-ship.

Log line

The log line, see Figure 161, would have consisted of 150 fathoms of well stretched lead line and calibrated while wet. When the log-ship is thrown overboard (Fig. 160), there needs to be sufficient 'stray-line' to clear the wake. At the point when the canvas ('butterfly') start mark passes, the sandglass is inverted. At every 47 feet 3 inches there is a leather thong marked progressively with 1, 2, etc knots. The number of thongs going out in 28 seconds is a direct reading of the ship's speed in knots. However, using the 14-second glass, the number of knots run out is doubled to know the speed; this avoids the need for an extra long log-line when exceeding 8 knots.[15] The log line is then 'jerked' to free the plug at the top of the log-ship before the line is recovered.

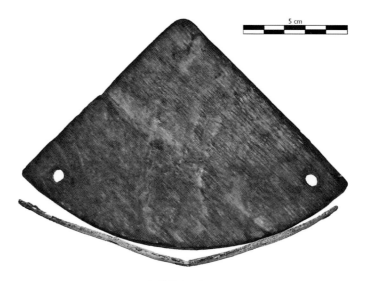

Figure 162. Log-ship Inv/87/086 (oak) and Inv/87/128 (lead strip). Photograph John Bingeman.

Figure 163. Log line reel end, Inv/88/275. Photograph John Bingeman.

The oak log line 'drum' end (Fig. 163) and protruding handle (not illustrated) were recovered. The rest of the drum had broken up and was not identified.

Figure 164. 305mm long sounding lead with three broad arrows, Inv/87/220.

Figure 165. 610mm long sounding lead (28lb) with three broad arrows. Its base has a deep pit for tallow to sample the seabed, Inv/88/059. Photograph J. A. Hewes.

Sounding leads

While underway, sounding leads were used to measure the depth of water under the ship, known as taking a 'sounding', by 'heaving the lead'. This was carried out from a small platform on the ship's side that supports the shrouds, and subsequently known as 'the chains'. In *Invincible*'s Court Martial proceedings,[16] the Board enquired "what was the depth when the order was given to go-about?" Thomas Gray, the leadsman, replied "7¼ fathoms". Nothing happened as the "tiller rope became foul"; *Invincible* ran aground despite attempts to 'back' the sails – the saga is recorded in Chapter 1.

Three sizes were recovered. The large sounding leads were around 25–28lb in weight, medium ones around 17lb, and the smaller ones from 12–14lb. See Figures 164 and 165.

List of sounding leads

Small:	Inv/87/146, 202 and 220. Inv/88/057
Medium:	Inv/88/045 and 052
Large:	Inv/87/154 and 185, Inv/88/014 and 059
	Total 10

Notes

1. Goodwin, P. *Sailing Man of War* 1650–1850, Conway Maritime Press, London 1987, 7–8.
2. NMM POR/D/9, dated 14th August 1747.
3. Bingeman, J. M., *et al. Copper and Other Sheathing in the Royal Navy*, IJNA (2000), 29.2: 218–229.
4. Goodwin, P. *The Influence of Iron in Ship Construction*; 1660 to 1830. MM (1998), 84.1: 26–40.
5. NMM POR/D/9 dated 14th August 1747.
6. B Sc (Hons) Applied Physics Project 1988 by I. Goodfellow, Supervisor: Dr R. Fenn, Portsmouth Polytechnic.
7. NA ADM 1/5297 6th March 1758
8. McGowan, A. 1999 *HMS Victory, Her Construction, Career and Restoration*, Chatham Publishing, London
9. Country Life Books, Nautical Terms Under Sail, entry: 05.02, London, 1978.
10. Boudriot, J. 1977 *Le Vaisseau de 74 Canons [The 74-gun Ship] en quatre tômes*, Collection Archéologiqie Naval Française, Paris, France, Vol. 2, 18.
11. *Ibid.,* p. 17.
12. HMSO, 1952, *Manual of Seamanship*, Vol. II, 97, London.
13. Portsmouth Polytechnic letter 7th February 1989 signed by Dr Brian Plunkett reporting findings.
14. After Kihlberg, *Lore of the Ships*, Nordbook, 1977: 228
15. HMSO, 1951, *Manual of Seamanship, Vol. II*, 608–9, London.
16. NA ADM 1/5297 dated 5th March 1758.

5. The Warship. Guns, Powder and Accoutrements. Army

Figure 166. *Powder barrel, height 20 inches (510mm), Inv/87/235. Photograph J. A. Hewes.*

Powder barrels

Invincible's Ordnance manifest listed a total of 300 powder barrels. Forty-eight whole barrels (Fig. 166) were recovered from the Forward Magazine. It was found that the 14 hazel bandings had no strength and the four copper bands had reacted with the gun powder turning them into a brittle purple copper oxide with little strength. Each barrel lid was made up from four strips of oak. I developed the technique of completely binding the barrel with light rope before knocking in the outer small strip of the lid. As the barrel was gently brought to the surface, and while passing the barrel to Arthur Mack, it was emptied of its contents. The sea around the boat would become completely black! The first attempt to recover a full barrel without draining was unsuccessful. It was much easier to conserve a barrel when in one piece with the lid removed, rather than reconstructing a barrel from pieces. The hazel banding quickly recovered its strength on drying. Samples of the powder were taken separately for analysis by the Portsmouth Polytechnic (later Portsmouth University).[1]

Figure 167. *Chris Underwood excavating in the forward magazine. Photograph Christopher Dobbs.*

Figure 168. *Powder barrel showing the mark 'G/IC'. Sketch John R. Terry.*

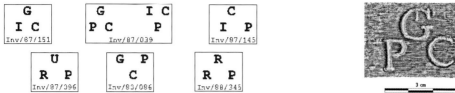

Figure 169. Drawing John P. Bethell.

Figure 170. A barrel lid showing the branded identification mark. Photograph John Bingeman.

In Figure 169, what these seven branded markings on barrel lids identify is not known. Markings G/PC and IC/P shown at top centre were both on barrel (Inv/87/039). Research at Woolwich Arsenal and the Museum of Naval Firepower, Priddy's Hard, Gosport, has not yet revealed an answer.

Besides these branded letter markings, the barrel lids all have broad arrow marks, and a single broad arrow was occasionally found on a barrel's side – see Figure 171.

The four copper bands on each powder barrel had reacted with the black powder to form a copper oxide. The resulting oxide was brittle and had little strength. In some cases a thin band of copper remained within the centre of the oxide. Figure 172's copper band was found away from the magazine and had little wastage. A second broadarrow was stamped on the opposite side.

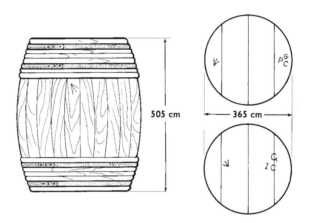

Figure 171. Powder barrel and lids from two different barrels. Drawing John R. Terry.

Figure 172. Powder barrel copper band's riveted joint. A broad arrow is just visible to the left of the rivet. Inv/90/003. Photograph John Bingeman.

Magazine powder box

The magazine powder box in Figure 173 was found in the Forward Hanging Magazine and at the time contained two copper powder-measures, see Figure 176. The purpose of the box was to receive the contents of a full powder barrel, so that copper scoops could be used to measure the powder required to fill paper, or in later periods flannel, cartridges.

The box's construction is in pine wood using tenon and mortise joints, while the handles and box base are secured using treenails (Fig. 175). Not using ferrous fastenings avoids the possible risk of fire from sparks.

Figure 176 is one of the two copper powder-measures found in the Magazine Powder Box. The copper had turned into a purple-coloured copper oxide. Conservation was unsuccessful. The reference number for the other measure was Inv/81/188.

Figure 173. The magazine powder box top measures 18 × 30 inches and stands 14 inches high, Inv/81/194. Photograph John Bingeman.

Figure 174. Treenails to secure the magazine powder box base. Photograph John Bingeman.

Figure 175. One of 30 treenails used to secure the powder box base. It measures 73 × 9 × 9mm, mainly 'squarish' with rounded corners. Reference: treenail from Inv/81/194. Photograph John Bingeman.

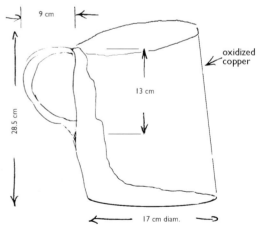

Figure 176. Drawing from John Bingeman's Diving Log 17/8/81, Inv/81/176.

Cartridge cases

The cartridge cases (Fig. 177) were among the hardest artefacts to conserve and a number were lost before a successful technique was established. Three sizes for the 9, 24 and 32-pounder cannons were recovered. Made from poplar wood, they were lathe turned and had substantial bases. Poplar is an absorbent wood and ideal for keeping powder dry. Among the fifty or so cases recovered a few had been repaired. Cartridge cases were sometimes known as 'cartridge boxes' or 'saltboxes', the latter presumably an abbreviation for the saltpetre (potassium nitrate) used to make gunpowder.

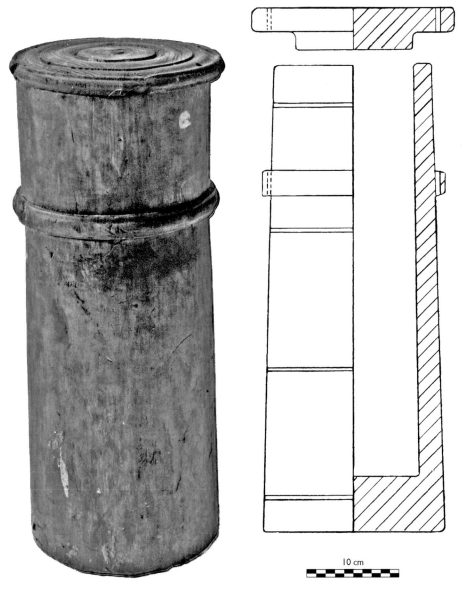

10 cm

Figure 177. Cartridge cases: left a typical 32-pounder case and right, drawing based on 32-pounder, Inv/88/105. Photograph Peter Hales, drawing John Bingeman.

The drawing in Figure 177 is based on Inv/88/105 showing the construction of a 32lb cartridge case standing 20 inches (508mm) high; it was unusual having four ornamental machined bands while the majority had none. The dimensions of the cases varied significantly.

It is interesting to note that these cartridge cases must have been highly valued; considerable trouble was taken to repair them. On the 'lip' reconstruction (Fig. 178), a white substance had been used as 'glue' before completing the repair with two brass staples. In Figure 179, a base has been repaired.

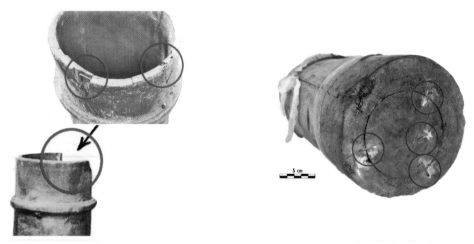

Figures 178 and 179. Lip repaired with two large brass staples 45mm long, Inv/88/155. Base repaired with four smaller brass staples, Inv/88/196.

Figure 180. A group of seven cartridge cases after conservation with a powder barrel on the right.

The cartridge cases had a thin rope lanyard threaded through two small holes directly opposite each other and tied together after passing round the underside of the rim. The rope lanyard then passed up and down through two similar holes in the lid – see Figure 181.

How were these cartridge cases carried? My assessment is that the thin 4mm hemp lanyard was there to keep the case and lid together. The lanyard is too weak to be used as a carrying handle. This contradicts the picture of the famous scene of Nelson collapsed on *Victory*'s deck in 1805 with a wounded powder monkey carrying a cartridge case by its lanyard (Fig. 182). Whether the method of carrying changed between 1758 and 1805 is open to conjecture. Certainly in 1758, the cartridge case must have been held against the body. If you imagine the powder monkey scampering from the hanging magazine below the waterline up ladders to the upper deck guns, the obvious way to run is to hold the case to the chest leaving his other arm free. This avoids the cartridge case swaying around on a thin lanyard. I don't know when the Trafalgar painting entitled the *Fall of Nelson*[2] was commissioned but it was probably many years after the event. I would also question its overall accuracy, for example: the large cutter in the centre top of this picture would have been hoisted out and trailed astern before going into action.

Captain Glascock, in his Naval Manual[3] published in 1836, comments that it has long been the practice to use white marline rope to keep the lid and the cartridge case together. *Invincible*'s cases in 1758 showed this to be true. He comments that in time of action the rope could become smeared

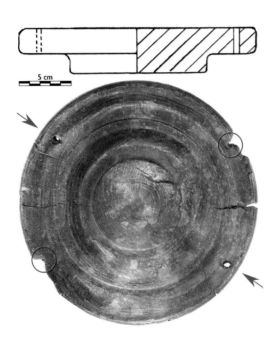

Figure 181. *Interestingly, there are four lanyard holes, the two original holes at 2 and 8 o'clock had broken through the rim and were replaced with holes at 4 and 10 o'clock. Photograph John Bingeman.*

Figure 182. *This extract from the famous picture at the National Maritime Museum, Greenwich may be incorrect; the 'powder monkey' is carrying the cartridge case by its lanyard rather than gripping it to his body. Photograph National Maritime Museum, Greenwich.*

with blood and powder creating the added risk of it becoming a quick match. The use of marline was therefore changed to 'leathern thongs'. Glascock refers to cartridge cases as 'Powder boxes'.

At the time of *Invincible*, gun charges were made up with powder inside paper 'bags' known as 'cartridges'. My other wreck, the 38-gun *Pomone* (1811) had used flannel 'bags' instead of paper which we found when emptying the contents of the 32lb carronade in Figure 196.

Hanging magazine

The hanging magazine racking was dismantled on the seabed without damage since pieces slotted together without any fastenings. Each piece is marked with a Roman numeral, making reassembly easy. At the base of the racks are two drawers thought to have contained moisture-absorbing charcoal. The magazine was re-assembled at Chatham Historic Dockyard to check for missing pieces, see Figures 183 and 184, and later put on public display, see Figure 188.

Invincible had two centre-line magazines, one forward and the other aft. They hung from the Orlop deck into the Hold, hence the name 'hanging' magazine. This allowed air to circulate, keeping the powder both dry and cool. Entry to the forward magazine was through the after part, known as the 'Annexe' which provided a general working area and where the gunpowder barrels were stored on wooden racks. Forward from this and at a slightly higher level was the 'Powder or Filling room' where gunpowder was filled into cartridges. A tasselled curtain, see sample in Figure 189, prevented any risk of flame or spark when filled cartridges were passed out in cartridge cases to boys known as 'powder monkeys', waiting in the Annexe.

Figure 183 and 184. Two views of the racking from the forward hanging magazine reassembled at Chatham Historic Dockyard. Three 32-pounder cartridge boxes are in the foreground. Photographs Chatham Historic Dockyard Trust.

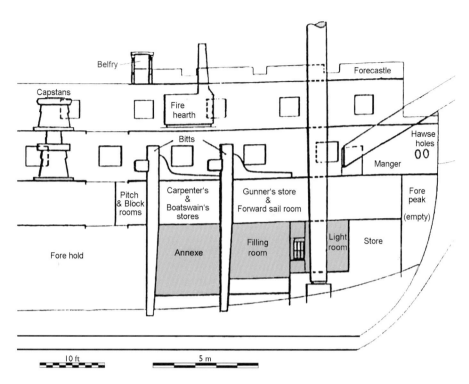

Figure 185. Invincible's *forward magazine arrangements. Drawing John P. Bethell.*

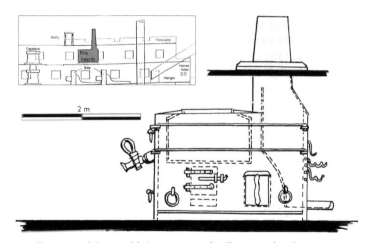

Figure 186. Invincible's *new type of galley stove fitted in 1756.*

Figure 185 is a diagram of *Invincible*'s forward magazine arrangements following her major refit at Portsmouth Dockyard between 1752 and 1756. The drawing also has the new type of galley stove fitted in 1756 on the Upper Deck and beneath the Forecastle Deck (Fig. 186). The stove was recovered at the time of her wrecking.

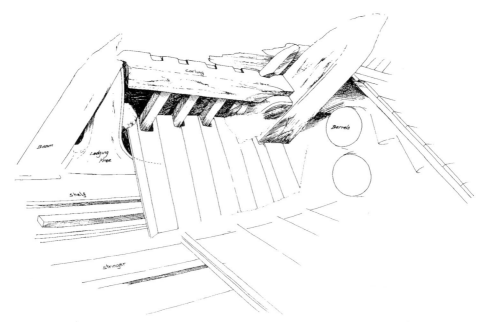

Figure 187. Annexe to the hanging magazine. Drawing Jonathan R. Adams.

Figure 188. Reconstruction of the Hanging Magazine, Chatham Historic Dockyard. Photograph John Bingeman.

Figure 187 is a drawing made underwater of the 'Annexe' to the Forward Hanging Magazine. On the far right, the square side of the 'Powder or Filling room' can be seen. The drawing was made after the racking had been recovered.

The structure from *Invincible*'s hanging magazine at Chatham Historic Dockyard was measured

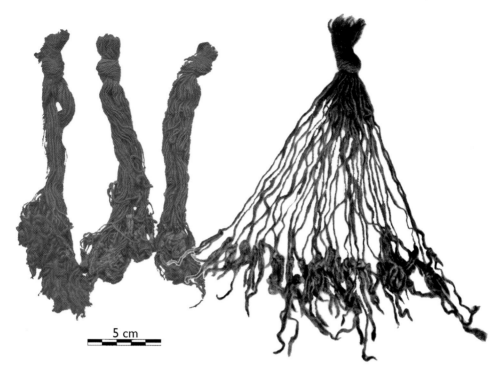

Figure 189. Magazine fire curtain tassels, Inv/84/312. Left: three examples from a bag of 96 tassels. Right: tassel opened out showing how the end fibres were further frayed out. Photographs: left three: John Bingeman, right: J. A. Hewes.

by Peter Goodwin, 'Curator and Keeper of HMS Victory', so that he could design a replica structure, since *Victory*'s hanging magazine had been removed many years before. The impressive replica was completed in time for the bi-centenary of the Battle of Trafalgar in 2005. This is one of many contributions made by the *Invincible* excavations to the restoration of *Victory* to her condition in 1805.

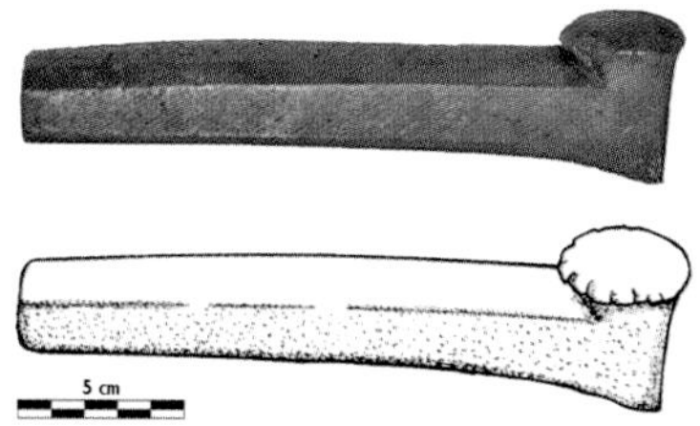

Woollen tassels (Fig. 189) were thought to have been used to edge the canvas curtain at the entrance to the magazine. Their purpose was to further assist in the prevention of fire.

It was a surprise to find metal tools in the magazine since Glascock's 1836 'General Directions for Magazine Tools'[5] warns against the use of any other than wooden setters for removal of copper hoops. Glascock further writes: 'The application of the gunmetal adze is a practice attended with considerable danger'.

Figure 190. Coopers' setter. Inv/80/275 and Inv/81/225 (both identical). Photograph Peter Hales, drawing John R. Terry.

Two bronze adzes (Fig. 191) and two brass coopers' setters (Fig. 190) were recovered in the vicinity of the forward hanging magazine. They would have been used to remove the hazel and copper banding from the powder barrels before emptying the barrels' contents into the magazine powder box (Fig. 173).

Figure 191 shows the head of one of the two cooper's adzes recovered and compares it with another

Iron conservation

Portsmouth City Museums Conservation Laboratory under the direction of the late Christopher O'Shea conserved *Pomone*'s three carronades – see Figure 197. The conservation process included stabilization in the hydrogen-reduction furnace. Sadly, the hydrogen-reduction furnace no longer exists and I am not aware of a similar installation in the United Kingdom for iron conservation. The results from this treatment have been exceptionally good and have lasted well with no apparent salt leaching or cracking of the iron. This treatment was used with great success on many of *Invincible*'s hand grenades; twenty-eight years later the grenades are still in pristine condition.

Figure 197. 32-pounder carronades before and after conservation in the hydrogen-reduction furnace – the left hand gun contained the gun contents (Fig. 196). Photograph Peter Hales.

Figure 198. The Pomone *(1811) 32-pounder carronade mounted on a replica gun carriage outside the Royal Naval Museum. This is the gun that contained its contents (Fig. 196).*

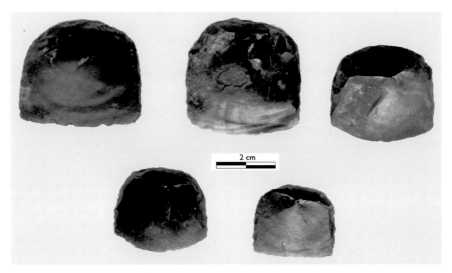

Figure 199. The five sizes of flints – 42, 38, 36, 32 and 26mm. Photograph John Bingeman.

Gun flints

Something in excess of 2,500 wedge-type gun flints were recovered. There were five sizes when measured across their striking edge (Fig. 199). The majority were of two sizes 38mm and 42mm. While there is no proof, it is thought likely that these two large sizes were for cannon locks under trial (see Fig. 228). *Invincible,* among thirteen ships, had been selected to trial cannon locks on her quarterdeck 9-pounder guns.[8]

Hand grenades

Thirty unbroken hand grenades were recovered, mainly lying on the surface in the bow area. A few were in the lead-lined storage box (Fig. 209). As previously stated, many of these grenades were successfully stabilised in the hydrogen-reduction furnace – see Figure 200. After conservation in the furnace, their original 'Inv' numbers had to be arbitrarily re-allocated to these grenades.

Naval hand grenades had developed in the 53 years between those recovered from *Invincible* and the 'standard' type recovered from *Pomone* (1811). The exterior surfaces of the *Pomone* grenades were much smoother (Fig. 202), with only a light horizontal mould mark. *Invincible's* grenades had a circular crevice where the molten metal had been fed through a 'feeder' pipe within the mould that was later removed, see cast mark in Figure 201. In addition, it had a distinct vertical mould mark vis-à-vis *Pomone* grenade's horizontal mould mark. The method of manufacture had clearly changed.

Concerning the wooden fuses, those of the *Pomone* were similar to those of the *Invincible* but shorter by 10mm and with square-cut ends instead of the angled ends found within *Invincible's* grenades (Fig. 203).

Grenade fuses had to be conserved separately. On the two beech fuses in Figure 203, the left had no marks but the right is marked 'XXVII' on its top rim. We are uncertain what this twenty-seven numeral indicates. If this was the intended fuse delay, it seems a rather lengthy period.

While no empty grenade shells were recovered, three unused beech fuses with solid bases were

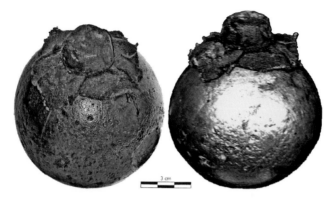

Figure 200. Two views of the same grenade. The fuse cover contains both the linen and canvas layers, Inv/80/052. Left photograph John Bingeman.

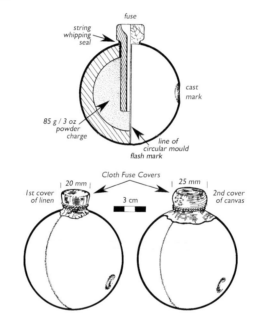

Figure 201. Illustrates grenade construction. Drawing John R. Terry.

found. The first fuse Figure 204 had the figure '75' and the second (Inv/83/132) had the figure '85', both figures being just below its 'neck'. Figures 205 and 206 are the third fuse plug with a 1½mm deep 'divot' above the figure '79'.

These examples of unused fuses confirm the method of filling by compressing the composition of saltpetre, sulphur and mealed powder into the fuse. Ten blows were applied using an 8½oz mallet to tamp the composition into the correct compression. These precise instructions were 'settled' in May 1752, presumably to provide consistent delay times – see Figure 207.[9] After charging, the fuse base was cut off.

The 18th century instructions always spelt 'fuze' with a 'z'. As a Royal Naval Cadet in the early 1950s, our Chief Petty Officer Gunner (Chief GI) told us that gunnery fuzes were spelt with a 'z' and electrical fuses with an 's'!

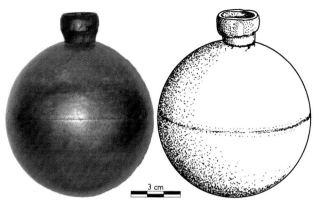

Figure 202. Pomone's 'standard' grenade. Photograph John Bingeman, drawing John R. Terry.

Figure 203. Wooden fuses from Invincible's *grenades. Photograph/drawing John Bingeman and Norman C. Lacey. 'Inv.' number not recorded.*

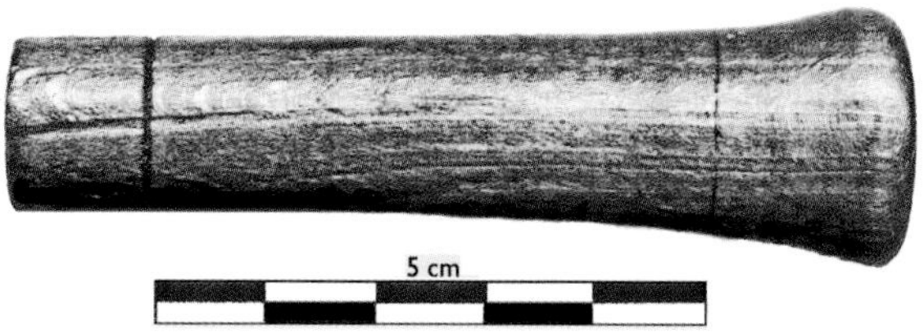

Figure 204. Unused Invincible *hand grenade fuse, Inv/81/201. Photograph John Bingeman.*

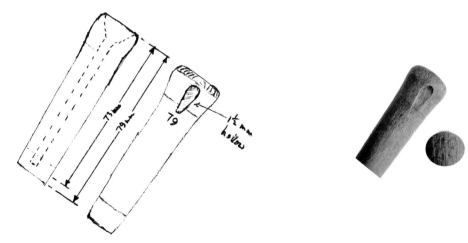

Figures 205 and 206. Showing the number on an unused fuse, Inv/88/064. Left: Drawing from John Bingeman's diving report dated the 23rd June 1988. Right: John Broomhead's photograph of the top half of the same fuse taken twenty years later in 2008. The number is barely legible.

Proportions of Fuzes as settled in May 1752.

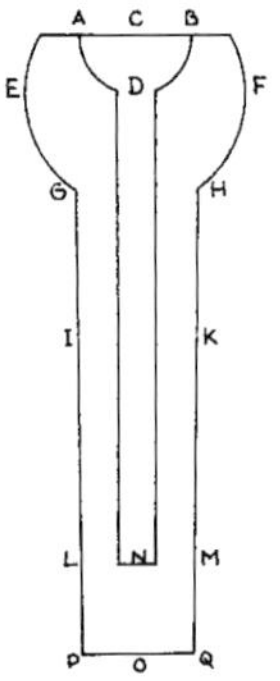

Proportions of Fuzes by Diameter of the Bore.			13 Inch	10 Inch	8 Inch	5½ Inch	4⅖ Inch	Hand	Musquet Diar^s	Musquet Inches
			Ins	Ins	Ins	Ins	Ins	Ins	Diar^s	Ins
Diameter of the Cup	AB	3 diam^rs	1·575	1·35	1·125	0·825	0·75	0·6	3	0·6
Depth of the Cup	CD	1½ diam^rs	0·787	0·675	0·562	0·412	0·375	0·3	1½	0·3
Greatest diameter of the Fuze	EF	4¾ diam^s	2·494	2·137	1·781	1·306	1·187	0·9	4	0·8
Exterior diameter of on Caliber below the Top of the Bore	GH	4 diam^rs	2·1	1·8	1·5	1·1	1·0	0·8	3½	0·7
Diameter of the middle of the Bore	IK	3⅓ diam^s	1·75	1·475	1·25	0·917	0·833	0·666	3	0·6
Diameter at the bottom of the Bore	LM	3 diam^rs	1·575	1·35	1·125	0·825	0·75	0·6	2¾	0·55
Diameter at the bottom of the Fuze	PQ	3 diam^rs								
Thickness of Wood at the Bottom of the Bore	NO	2 diam^rs	1·05	0·9	0·75	0·55	0·5	0·4	2	0·4
Diameter of the Bore in Inches			0·525	0·45	0·375	0·275	0·25	0·2		0·2
Length of the Bore in Inches	DN		8·4	7·2	6·375	4·4	3·5	2·25		2·0
Length of the Bore in its own Diameter or Calibre			16	16	17	16	14	11¼	10	
External length of the Fuze	CO		10·237	8·775	7·687	5·362	4·375	2·95		2·7
External length of the Fuze in Diameters			19½	19½	20½	19½	17½	14¾	13½	

Figure 207. Table showing fuse dimensions.

Besides the grenades and fuses already described, a single example of a different type was recovered at 'The Needles' wreck site. Perhaps the grenade (Fig. 208) was experimental. Its fuse (illustrated) was 45mm long with a coarse Acme (nearly square) thread which disintegrated. The grenades' fuse hole is larger with a diameter of 27mm compared to the 'standard' versions 17mm diameter. The fuse hole is concave between its top and bottom, possibly designed to hold a wooden plug which is thought to have had a matching female Acme thread that also disintegrated. The grenade body was in a fragile condition, most of the iron had leached out, leaving a light, practically all-carbon, shell. The shell was treated in the hydrogen-reduction furnace to stabilise the corrosion products but was slightly 'over cooked' causing it to distort. This has not unduly affected the size of the fuse hole.

Figure 208. Pomone*'s unusual experimental(?) grenade. Photograph John Bingeman.*

A few of *Invincible*'s thirty hand grenades were found in a five sided lead-lined storage box (Fig. 209). It was recovered when protruding out of the seabed (Fig. 210) attached to dislodged hull

Figure 209. Storage box for hand grenades, width 660mm, height 242mm, Inv/87/028. Photograph John Bingeman.

Figure 210. Grenade box on seabed before excavation on 6th June 1987. The grenades had been previously recovered. Photograph John Broomhead.

structure close to the bow and level with the Orlop deck. We speculate that this unusually shaped box was specially built to fit the compartment. The grenades in the box were all primed ready for use.

Slow-match pouch

Figures 211 and 212 illustrate the slow-match circular pouch made of two layers of 'fearnought' cloth containing a 14 foot length of slow-match wick. The wick will pull out from the centre; the Licensee has tested this principle and it really works. In the 'Fighting Tops' a marine would have used this pouch to light grenades before throwing them during a close-ship engagement. As the slow-match wick burnt, the marine would pull the wick out to keep the burning end just outside the fearnought pouch.

Fearnought is woollen cloth severely shrunk to give a very close weave. The Royal Navy used fearnought-suits for heat protection; additional protection is given if the suit is first damped and kept damp by spray when fire-fighting.[11]

Figure 211. Slow-match pouch. When recovered the stitching had split revealing the slow-match wick, Inv/87/075. Photograph Peter Hales.

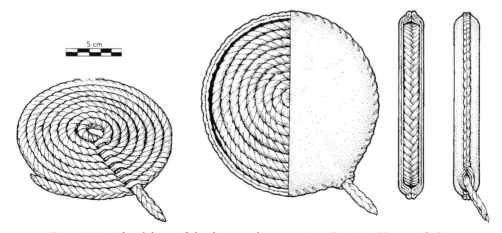

Figure 212. A breakdown of the slow-match construction. Drawing Norman C. Lacey.

Leather buckets

Thirty-six leather buckets were recovered from the Gunner's store, many packed inside each other. It is thought they would have held water for sponging out cannon after each round had been fired. This assumption is made firstly because they were found in the Gunner's Store and secondly one had been painted silver with 'G2R, No18 and 1757' – almost certainly belonging to Gun No18 gun's crew (Fig. 217).

The hide used for the bucket, see Figure 213, was about 5mm thick and the bucket stood 0.260m (10.2 inches) high with internal diameters at base 0.160m (6.3 inches) and top 0.215m (8.4 inches). The top was made circular by a hazel grommet secured with an exterior strap some 32mm wide. Hand stitched, the base is reinforced by a cross of leather straps within the raised base, see Figure 216. The majority had a scratched broad arrow as illustrated; others had a branded broad arrow 18mm long, and one of these also had an inspector's mark of a crown above a 6 – Figure 214.

The two ferrous rings that join the leather handle to the bucket's reinforced rim had corroded away on all thirty-six buckets. There was one exception, on one side only, tar had covered the ring and preserved it on bucket Inv/83/137 – see Figure 215.

Figure 213. *Leather bucket is complete except for replaced handle rings. Photograph Peter Hales.*

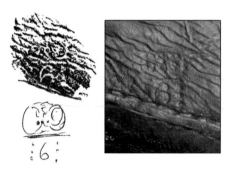

Figure 214. *A rubbing, drawing and photograph of the inspector's mark on leather bucket, Inv/81/124. Rubbing and drawing John Bingeman, photograph J. A. Hewes.*

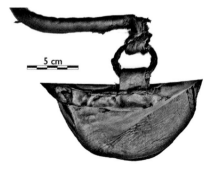

Figure 215. *The surviving iron ring on leather bucket, Inv/83/137. Photograph John Bingeman.*

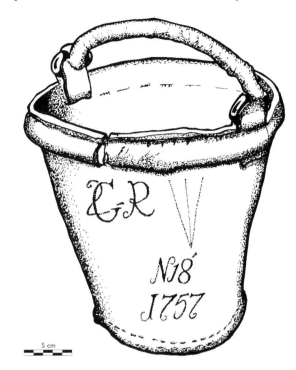

Figure 216. Reinforcement of the bucket's base, Inv/83/137. Photograph John Bingeman.

Figure 217. 'Nº18' Gun crew's leather bucket, Inv/83/022. Drawing John R. Terry.

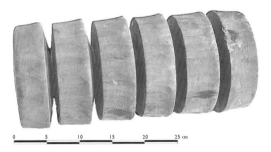

Figure 218. Spool of six tampions for 32lb calibre gun. Photograph Peter Hales.

Tampi ons

Figure 218 illustrates 32-pounder tampions in spools of six. They were machined in a lathe from a single piece of pine without a final parting cut. The spools were all for 32-pounder guns and only a single spool for a 24-pounder.

Only a single 9lb-tampion was recovered (Inv/80/234).

32-pounder spools: Inv/80/203, 209, 213 84/258, 300, 316 and 317.

Figure 220 shows a repair to a 24-pounder tampion's outer face where cracks had been plugged with pieces of filler wood and mortar paste.

Figure 219. Gunner's store. The underwater photograph shows a 10 inch double block, two sponge 'cylinders', a rammer head, and a spool of tampions. Photograph John Broomhead.

Figure 220. 24-pounder tampion repair, Inv/86/102. Photographs John Bingeman.

Sponge 'cylinders'

Spare sponge 'cylinders' (Fig. 221) were recovered from the gunner's store. The cylinders have a hollow centre to take a shaft and would have formed the 'body' to take a sheepskin covering. Three sizes were recovered. The wood was very soft and shrank during conservation, so exact dimensions were never fully established. These readings were taken at the time of recovery:

24-pounder (Inv/84/174) – length 225mm, diameter 115mm and stamped '24'.
32-pounder (Inv/84/222) – length 245mm, diameter 140/125mm (oval in shape).

After conservation, their overall length remained the same but their diameters had reduced by around 20%.

List of sponge 'cylinders
9-pounder   Inv/84/359.
24-pounder   Inv/84/174, 262, 288, 295, 299, 309, 310 and 363.
32-pounder   Inv/84/222, 263, 274, 279, 289, 298 and 362.

Rammer heads

Besides the 9-pounder rammer head in Figure 222, all three calibre guns sizes were recovered. Figure 223 is an example of how the identification size was punched on the top of each rammer head and on the underside there were 7mm high 'I' marks. What the latter stood for is unknown.

A bundle of shafts for rammer heads were riddled with 6/7mm diameter teredo worm holes and fell to pieces.

Figure 221. *24lb and 32lb sponge carriers after conservation. Photograph John Bingeman.*

Figure 222. *9-pounder rammer head, Inv/80/152 Photograph Peter Hales.*

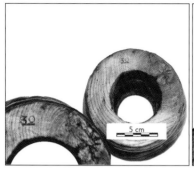
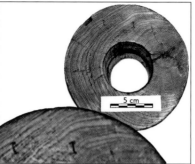

Figure 223. Markings on a 32-pounder rammer head's top and base. Left: top shows the '32'. Right: base shows the two 'T's, Inv/84/246. Photographs John Bingeman.

Figure 224. Pine vent stopper, length 47mm, maximum diameter 14mm, Inv/85/008. From: Heart of Oak – A Sailors Life in Nelson's Navy by James P. McGuane. © 2002 James P. McGuane. Used by permission of W. W. Norton & Company.

Rammer head sizes
9-pounder – 98mm (3.8 inches) diameter
24-pounder – 138mm (5.4 inches) diameter
32-pounder – 156mm (6.1 inches) diameter

Vent stopper

A vent stopper would have been used to plug the cannon's vent hole during sponging out after firing the gun. The example (Fig. 224) recovered had the tapered end tip broken off.

Aprons of lead

An 'Apron of Lead' is, to quote Blackmore, "a piece of square plate of lead that covers the vent of a cannon, to keep the charge dry, and the vent clean and open".[12] Although it is known that *Invincible* was trialling cannon locks (see Chapter 1) on her Quarterdeck 9-pounder guns, the only 'aprons' found were all flat rather than with the 'hump' required to cover a lock. Figure 225 shows the two sizes of 'aprons' recovered.

Small: 140 × 140 mm (5½ × 5½ inch)
Large: 254 × 302 mm (10 × 12 inch)
       254 × 324 mm (10 × 12¾ inch)
(There were some slight variations to these dimensions.)

All 'aprons' were 3mm thick and had four 7mm holes for securing a rope lanyard. The larger size fits the description in Blackmore;[13] the smaller is a slight variant from Blackmore's quoted size of 6 × 4½ inches.

List of aprons of lead
Small: Inv/80/065, 128, 302, 304 and 312, and 81/036
Large: Inv/80/016(two), Inv/83/023, 038, 072, 073, and 074 Inv/83/024 (without securing holes)

Although we had found no 'humped' aprons for cannon locks on *Invincible*,[14] I had previously recovered two while excavating *Pomone* (1811) wreck site at The Needles. While not part of the Book, I think the subject worthy of inclusion because it describes items that were possibly carried by *Invincible*

Figure 225. 5½ × 5½ inch and 10 × 12 inch 'aprons of lead'. Photographs Peter Hales.

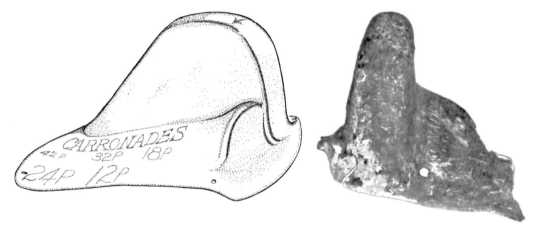

Figure 226. Pomone *(1811) 'apron of lead' for the cannon lock of a 32-pounder carronade. Drawing John R. Terry, photograph John Bingeman.*

Figure 227. A well used 'apron' from one of Pomone's *18-pounder guns. Photograph John Bingeman.*

although not recovered. Figure 226 shows a drawing and photograph of a *Pomone* apron designed to cover cannon locks on her 32-pounder carronades.[15] The figures on the carronade apron drawing shows that they could be used for all calibres from 12lb to 42lbs. Figures 229 and 230 illustrate two types of cannon lock recovered from *Pomone*.

Also recovered from the *Pomone* site was another apron with a similar hump – see Figure 227. This apron would have come from one of *Pomone*'s 18-pounder cannons although, due to surface erosion, the only remaining visible mark is for a 12-pounder gun.

Pomone's *cannon lock*

Two locks were recovered from the *Pomone* (1811) wreck site – see Figures 229 and 230. The hatched area in Figure 228 shows what the lock would have looked like before its iron had corroded away after 171 years underwater. The knapping of flints had changed since 1758, and they were now 'platform' shaped to improve gripping in the jaws of both cannon locks and muskets. A thin piece of leather was found covering the top, back, and bottom of this platform flint. Inside the second lock was marked with a small crown above a '3' – this may have been an inspector's mark.

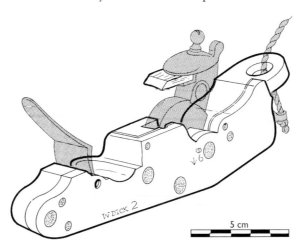

Figure 228. Pomone's *cannon lock manufactured in London by W. Dick. Drawing John R. Terry.*

Figures 229 and 230. Interiors of the Pomone's *locks after stabilization by Portsmouth City Museums Conservation Laboratory. Left: 'Dick' lock. Right the second lock recovered with an 18-pounder while still attached to its breech. Photographs Peter Hales.*

Lantern 'glass'

A thin piece of horn measuring 82 × 110mm (Inv/86/067) was thought to have been a pane for use in a lantern. It was recovered in the vicinity of the Gunner's Store and above the forward magazine. Other pieces of thin horn were recovered but disintegrated.

Trucks

Thirteen spare gun carriage trucks were found in a forward store. Their sizes were 21, 19 and 16 inch outside diameters. While the two 21-inch wheels had no markings, the 19-inch wheel had '32·P·19·F' and the 16-inch wheels had '24·P·16·H' (Fig. 231). The markings of '32·P' and '24·P' would indicate the guns' calibre. The markings of '19' and '16' indicate the outside diameter of the wheels in inches. The markings 'F' and 'H' indicate the positions (Fore and Hind) of the wheels on the gun carriage.

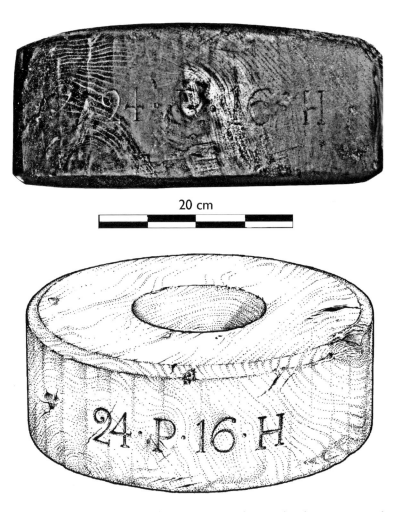

20 cm

Figure 231. The 24-pounder gun carriage truck, Inv/90/060. Photograph John Bingeman, drawing Norman C. Lacey.

Figure 232. Stool is marked '9 P 8½ F' indicating that it is for a 9-pounder gun with an 8½ foot barrel, Inv/84/302. Photograph Peter Hales.

Figure 233. Close-up of Fig. 232, the '9 P 8½ F' is visible. Photograph Peter Hales.

Figure 234. Concretions from the securing bolts, a broad arrow and the 'inspector's mark', Inv/84/302. Photograph Peter Hales.

Figure 235. The 'JMB' inspector's mark enlarged. Photograph Peter Hales.

Stool beds

Ten spare stool beds for gun carriages were recovered from the gunner's store. Figures 232 to 235 illustrate the structure of the 9-pounder that had the manuscript letters 'JMB', which prompted other divers present to accuse the Licensee of stamping his own initials on the stool bed while on the seabed! More seriously, these initials could either have originated from the manufacturer or possibly an inspector's mark (Fig. 235).

List of stool beds

9-pounder	Inv/84/302
24-pounder	Inv/84/196, 197, 198, 277 and 368
	Severely degraded: Inv/84/207 and 277
32-pounder	Inv/84/236 and 267

Elevating quoins

Two types of quoin were recovered. Figure 236 was for a 32-pounder gun and stamped with *Invincible*'s name. This was necessary since *Invincible* was built by the French and her gun ports were not to British standard dimensions and needed special quoins. All British built ships had standard-sized gun ports so that ordnance could be transferred from one ship to another. The only other example known to the Licensee, of a quoin with a ship's name, comes from the Spanish *San Josef*. It is stamped 'San Joseph' with an inverted '32P' – see Figure 237. The 112 gun three-decker *San Josef* had been captured by Admiral Lord Nelson at the battle of Cape St Vincent in 1797. The quoin is in the Valhalla Collection on Tresco in the Isles of Scilly, an outstation of the National Maritime Museum.

Figure 236. The 32-pounder gun carriage elm quoin special to Invincible, Inv/90/062. Photograph John Bingeman, drawings Norman C. Lacey.

The other *Invincible* quoin is a simple elm wedge (Inv/90/063), measuring 325 × 190mm and tapering from 105 to 58mm. It has an off-centre 17mm diameter hole, possibly to pass a rope, and a branded broad arrow 20mm in length.

Shot

Comparatively few shot were recovered during the eleven years of excavations. In 1989 a patch of 32lb shot became exposed on the north-east side of Trench 'JJ'. These shot were not disturbed and left in situ.

One unusual 9lb iron shot (Fig. 238) thought to be a 'langrel or expanding shot' was known to have been in use during the 18th century.[17] The word 'expanding' meant it fractured on impact which helps to explain why it partly broke up shortly after recovery. It contained a number of layers of circular metal 'dice' similarly arranged like those in a flat box of cheese. This arrangement can be seen in the Licensee's tracing

Figure 237. San Joseph (Josef) Quoin, circa 1797. Photograph National Maritime Museum, Greenwich.

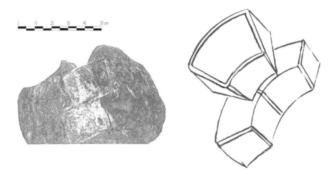

Figure 238. The internal appearance of this unusual 9lb shot. Left: Photograph Portsmouth Polytechnic. Right: Licensee's sketch to indicate two layers of dice and their oxide coating.

of his rough sketch made at the time of recovery. Each dice or cube had a distinct outside coating of oxide which, when first examined, looked like and bent like a thin layer of lead. Portsmouth Polytechnic's examination concluded that the cubes or dice were 'grey' cast iron and were encased in a heavily corroded wrought iron shell.[18]

Wicker baskets

Sixteen wicker baskets (Fig. 239) were recovered. Whether these were Gunner's stores or not, they are included in this section because they were recovered from the Gunner's Store. One of these baskets was full of split ash blocks.

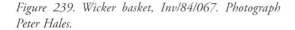

Figure 239. Wicker basket, Inv/84/067. Photograph Peter Hales.

Figure 240. Ash block measuring 220 × 65 × 25mm. Photograph John Bingeman.

Figure 241. An elm 1690mm Samson bar or crow bar, the handle is rather thinner than it would have been originally due to gribble worm attack, Inv/84/065. Photograph Geoff Lee.

Split blocks

Figure 240 is one of the numerous ash blocks recovered. The majority were found loose, though a number were found in a wicker basket in the Gunner's store. One theory was that these blocks were used in conjunction with a Samson bar (see Fig. 241) when levering gun carriages during aiming. Equally they could have been used as logs for the new type of galley range (see Fig. 186) fitted in the 1752–56 Refit at Portsmouth and recovered during salvage operations in 1758. However the former use seems more likely since these blocks were consistently the same size and seem a little too small for burning.

Evidence of the Army onboard *Invincible*

Invincible's Log records that two Lieutenants, a Sergeant and 42 soldiers from Cornwallis's Regiment (24th Regiment of Foot) boarded *Invincible* on the 10th February 1758.[19] A letter of March 1758[20] instructs that the mattresses of the 34th and 37th Regiments of Foot were to be removed from the wreck of the *Invincible*. These two records confirm the presence of troops onboard *Invincible*.

An earlier letter[21] from Barrington (Secretary of War) to Admiral Boscawen dated 10th February says two companies of the 2nd Battalions of the 34th and 37th Regiments of Foot were to travel with the Fleet to North America. When the 2nd Battalion of the 34th was formed from the 1st Battalion it was numbered the 67th, and was one of General Wolfe's Regiments. Similarly, the 2nd Battalion of the 37th was numbered the 55th and was Brigadier-General George Augustus Howe's Regiment. Some of his Regiment were already in America.

Another Barrington letter[22] to Boscawen dated 13 February informs him that fifteen unattached officers were to go onboard the Fleet as reinforcements. Could these be the fifteen supernumeries on *Invincible*'s Muster List? During excavations, various regimental buttons were recovered. If the supernumeries were the unattached officers could they have been the owners of these buttons? A separate Interim Report on military buttons was published in the *International Journal of Nautical Archaeology*[23] in 1997, and is now repeated at Appendix B.

Cartouche boxes

The posh name for these curved wooden cartridge boxes was a 'cartouche'; they were also referred to as 'cartridge pouches'. The first cartouche cover (Fig. 242) was embossed with 'G2R'. The '2' of the 'G2R' was inscribed within the 'G' and similar to the Royal ciphers seen on cannon. The second cover (Inv/89/271), found in the stern area of the wreck site, had a similar but gold-leaf embossed 'GR' with no "2" (Fig. 243). The third and fourth covers had no markings.

Figure 244 is the sketch of the third cartouche box with a plain cover and illustrates how the box was secured to the soldier's body.

A fourth plain leather cover (Inv/84/179) was recovered without its wooden box. It measured 250 × 150mm.

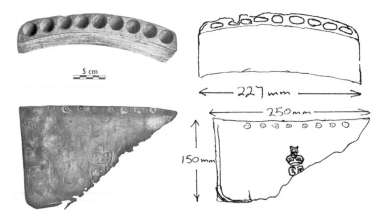

Figure 242. Cartouche, Inv/80/004 (box) and 005 (cover). Photograph Peter Hales, sketch Simon Aked.

Figure 243. Cartouche leather cover, Inv/89/271. Photograph John Bingeman.

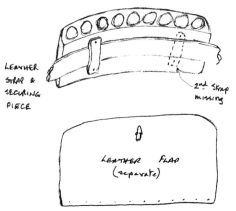

Figure 244. Cartouche box, Inv/88/088 and belt and cover, Inv/88/089. Sketch from John Bingeman's diving log for 28th June 1988.

North American changes to Army uniform

Brigadier-General, The Honourable George Augustus Howe, an illegitimate first cousin of King George II, was credited with introducing green (rather than red) uniforms with brown felt hats. It made the soldiers less conspicuous when fighting the Indians and French through the woods in North America. He also cut down musket barrels for more rapid response in close combat. Among the few personal artefacts recovered was a Howe signet ring (Fig. 245). It may have been in baggage intended for George Augustus Howe, already in North America; he was later killed during a skirmish at Ticonderoga on the 6th July 1758. Alternatively, it may have been for his youngest brother Sir William Howe, a Major who could have been one of the fifteen supernumeries taking passage. Certainly, William Howe was part of the Second Louisbourg Expedition, and subsequently became the Army Commander-in-Chief North

Figure 245. The Howe signet ring, Inv/83/199.

America when his elder brother Admiral Earl Richard Howe was the Naval Commander-in-Chief, North America. It is the only time in British military history that two brothers have been Commanders-in-Chief of their respective services in the same field of operations.

The 2nd Battalion of the 37th Regiment of Foot had their mattresses onboard *Invincible*.[24] This was George Augustus Howe's Regiment which might further reinforce the theory that the ring belonged to him. The 2nd Battalion of the 37th was also numbered the 55th Regiment of Foot which adds to the confusion in regimental numbers.

I was able to verify the ownership of the ring. Long-term family connections with the Howe family gave me the opportunity of visiting their ancestral home at Penn House, with its impressive collection of paintings and artefacts covering over 200 years of their family history. The Earl and Countess kindly showed us various relevant books and documents and confirmed that the signet ring depicts one of the earlier crests of the family. Unfortunately, we were unable to see the famous diamond-studded ceremonial sword presented to Admiral of the Fleet, Earl Howe (1726–99) as it was on loan to the National Maritime Museum.

Soldiers' uniforms

A soldier's felt hat (Fig. 246) was the first artefact recovered by the Licensee when he was being guided around the site for the first time in April 1980 by John Broomhead. The hat was lying on the seabed surface and likely to have been washed away. Subsequently, a similar felt hat was recovered in a rather degraded condition (Inv/86/116).

A single boot (Fig. 247) was recovered in pieces as well as a khaki coloured stocking (Fig. 248) with a neat darn. Close by there was a matching ball of wool (Inv/86/183).

Brigadier-General George Augustus Howe, as previously stated, was one of the officers responsible for adapting army uniforms for fighting the Indians and French in the North American campaigns. Appropriately, Gerry Embleton's impression in Figure 249 chose a private from Howe's 55th Regiment of Foot. Although not shown here, the red uniforms were later dyed to brown and dark green. During *Invincible*'s excavations similar hats, cartridge cartouches, and a boot were recovered.

Besides the soldier's felt hat, a heavy leather cap with peak was also introduced. Major George Scott, Commanding Officer of the Provisional Light Infantry Battalion who had distinguished himself

Figure 246. Soldier's felt hat, Inv/80/001. Photograph Peter Hales.

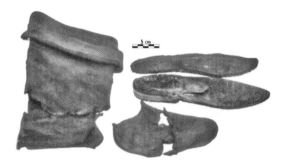

Figure 247. Soldier's boot, Inv/88/122 and 129. Photograph John Bingeman.

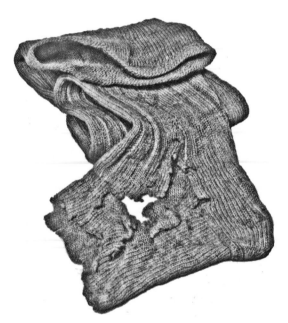

Figure 248. Soldier's stocking, Inv/86/182.

Figure 249. A private from Brigadier-General Howe's 55th Regiment of Foot, circa 1758. Image by Gerry Embleton, from Wolfe's Army (Men-at-Arms 48) *by Robin May © Osprey Publishing Ltd.*

during the 1758 Louisbourg landings, proposed other reforms to uniforms for the Light Infantry. A quote from Major Scott's letter:

> 'The Leather Cap', he argued, 'if properly jack't and made of good Leather is intended to fend off the blow of a Scalping-Ax or Firelock. It is also better adapted to the Hood of a Cloke (cloak) than a Hatt and will keep its form'.[25]

Remember at the time, the English were fighting not only the French but also the Indians with their scalping axes!

Figure 250 is the hat that Major George Scott is referring to. The cap's leather thickness was about 7mm and had a slightly domed brass 'button' (diameter 28mm) at the top (Fig. 251). A leather crescent shaped hat peak (Inv/89/147) with stitch marks on the inside of the curve was recovered a year later. The cap and its peak were not put together to see if the stitching matched because research had not been undertaken and its significance was not appreciated.

The Major's portrait and leather cap are shown in Figures 252 and 253.

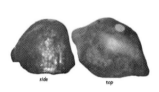

Figure 250. *The leather cap with brass central 'button', Inv/88/229.*

Figure 251 *The brass slightly domed cap button, and reverse side showing securing eyelet, diameter 28mm, Inv/88/229.*

Figures 252 and 253. *Copley's portrait of Major George Scott, circa 1758–59. The Major has a similar leather cap in his right hand. The peak can be seen but his hand is over the 'button'.*

Figure 254. Knitted woollen 'Monmouth' cap, Inv/84/024. From: Heart of Oak – A Sailors Life in Nelson's Navy *by James P. McGuane. © 2002 James P. McGuane. Used by permission of W. W. Norton and Company*

Figure 254 is a knitted woollen headdress known as a 'Monmouth cap' that could have been worn by either a sailor or soldier. It has a pom-pom on top and horizontal lines making a striped pattern.

Musket shot

Something in excess of 12,000 musket and pistol shot were recovered during the eleven years of excavations. Their diameters were found to be in three sizes: 0.521, 0.603, and 0.686 inches (13.22, 15.40, and 17.50mm). These are 'mid' average diameters. A more detailed study using random groups from each of the three sizes was carried out by a student at Portsmouth Polytechnic.[26]

Among them were examples of a shot with a special 'lip' for binding into a cartridge. Also recovered was a wooden former (Inv/80/278) for making musket cartridges; a second former was recovered (Inv/88/226) but did not respond well to conservation. See Figure 255.

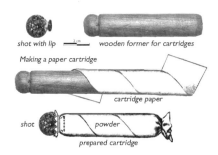

Figure 255. Illustration shows the 'lipped' musket shot (17.88mm/0.705 inch diameter) being made into a paper cartridge using a wooden former, Inv/80/278. Drawing John P. Bethell.

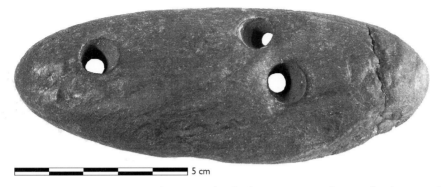

Figure 256. Rope tensioner (120 × 45mm) made of oak, Inv/80/010. Photograph John Broomhead.

Figure 257. Toggle made of oak, length 77mm, max diameter 26mm, Inv/84/205. Photograph John Bingeman.

Army stores

It is not known whether the Army was carrying any tentage for use during the Louisbourg Expedition. However, three beech tent pegs (Inv/84/004 and 87/059 and 060), length 377mm were recovered as well as the pierced well-worn oak block (Fig. 256) and an oak toggle (Fig. 257). It is thought that the former could have been used for tensioning guy ropes.

Notes

1. Portsmouth Polytechnic Fourth Year BSc Applied Physics Project 1990. Student Sean Leonard, Supervisor Dr R. Fenn.
2. Dighton, Denis, *The Battle of Trafalgar, 21st October 1805: Fall of Nelson*, NMM negative no. A8019
3. Glascock, W. N., 1836, *The Naval Service or Officers' Manual*, Vol. 2, 26. Saunders and Otley, London.
4. Lavery, B., 1987. *The Royal Navy's First Invincible*. Portsmouth, 76.
5. Gascock,W. N., 1836. *The Naval Service or Officers' Manual*, Vol. 2, 7. Saunders and Otley, London.
6. *Ibid*.
7. Bingeman, J, *Interim Report H. M. Ships Assurance-Pomone Excavations 1979*, NMM ref: PBN 4517 930.23(204).
8. NA ADM 2/219 letter dated 21 October 1755.
9. Caruana, A. B., *British Artillery Ammunition 1780*, Museum Restoration Service, Ontario, Canada, 1979, 23.
10. *Ibid*.
11. Admiralty, *Manual of Seamanship*, Vol. 2, 43, HMSO, London, 1952.
12. Blackmore, H. L., 1976. *The Armouries of the Tower of London*, HMSO, London.

13. *Ibid.*
14. NA ADM 2/219 letter dated 21 October 1755.
15. Smith, R. D. (ed.), *British Naval Armaments*, Royal Armouries 1979, 43.
16. '*Valhalla*' The Tresco Ships' Figurehead Collection, National Maritime Museum, 1984, exhib. no. 54
17. Blackmore, H. L., 1976, *The Armouries of the Tower of London*, HMSO, London.
18. Portsmouth Polytechic Fourth year BSc Applied Physics Project 1990. Student Sean Leonard, Supervisor Dr R. Fenn.
19. NA ADM 1/471
20. NA ADM 2/522
21. WO 4/55 dated 10 February 1758.
22. WO 4/55 dated 13 February 1758.
23. *International Journal of Nautical Archaeology* (1997) **26**.1:39–50.
24. NA ADM 2/522
25. I. M. McCulloch and T. J. Todish, *British Light Infantryman of the Seven Years' War*, Osprey Publishing, Oxford, UK, 2004, 11.
26. Portsmouth Polytechnic Fourth Year BSc Applied Physics Final Year Report 1985. Student T. M. O'Brian, Supervisor Dr B. A. Plunkett.

6. Domestic, Personal and Miscellaneous

Introduction

This Chapter contains many domestic items that are difficult to collate in an orderly fashion.

Pewter

Two pewter plates (Inv/89/269 and 307) and a porringer (Fig. 260) were recovered from the stern area of the ship.

The most interesting plate (Fig. 259) had inscribed on the rim: 'Invincible to Service April 23 1757'. This was the date when *Invincible* completed her 2-year refit at Portsmouth Dockyard and may have been a presentation plate to mark her completion. On the base was the faint pewter mark of 'Samuel Ellis' and his four Guild touch marks. This was similar to an Ellis touch mark illustrated in Figure 259. Samuel Ellis was a prolific London pewterer who worked from 1721 to 1765.

Since 1989 when the plate was recovered and conserved, it has oxidized and the inscription and touch marks have become barely discernable. Close scrutiny still reveals 'April 23 1757' and the Ellis guild marks.

Figure 258. Pewter plate, Inv/89/269, pewter spoon, Inv/89/226, wine bottle, Inv/89/169 and wooden tankard, Inv/89/173. Sketch by John R. Terry.

Figure 259. The 'presentation' pewter plate diameter 235mm, Inv/89/269. Photograph John Bingeman.

Figure 260. Pewter porringer, Inv/89/328. diameter 135mm. Photograph John Bingeman.

Figure 261. Coconut cup, Inv/81/218. Photographs Geoff Lee.

Coconut cup

When *Invincible* was wrecked, one half of a well polished coconut shell (Fig. 261) had floated and become trapped under the timbers of the Gun deck. There was little doubt that it had been used as a cup. The suggestion that it might have had a silver rim can be discounted.

Bottles

While sherds of numerous broken bottles were recovered, a total of eleven wine bottles and four half-size wine bottles (Figures 262 and 263) were recovered and these were mainly found during excavations of the ship's stern. Other bottles/jars are illustrated in Figures 265 to 268.

Wine bottle:
       Inv/85/013 and Inv/86/163
       Inv/89/114, 137, 169, 213, 237, 239, 258, 282 and 286
Half bottle:
       Inv/89/002, and 075
       Inv/90/064
Mallet bottle:
       Inv/88/253 – diameter 115mm, height 124mm. Figure 262.
       (The Diving boat's log records it as a small 'onion bottle'.)

Invincible bottles all pre-dated 1758. Various authorities suggest that this shape of bottle came into use in the 1780s. A time capsule like *Invincible* provides positive dating.

    One bottle (Fig. 264) contained berries which were identified as Juniper (*juniperus communis*). These berries were used to flavour gin and had medicinal uses to kill intestinal worms, and cure both 'fluxes' and dropsy. *Invincible*'s berries, measuring 6 to 9mm in diameter, were compared with specimens from the Hampshire downland and were found to be identical in structure. This research was carried out by James Plunkett under the direction of his late father, Dr Brian A. Plunkett, at Portsmouth Polytechnic.[1]

Figure 262. Left: mallet bottle, height 124mm, Inv/88/253; right: wine bottle, height 250mm, Chatham INV.429. Photographs Geoff Lee.

Figure 263. A comparison of the full-size (Inv/89/114) and half-size (Inv/90/064) bottles. Heights 250 and 205mm. Photograph John Bingeman.

Figure 264. A wine bottle with berries, Inv/88/286. Photograph John Bingeman.

Figures 265 and 266. Left: small case bottle, Inv/89/263; right: medicine phial, height 70mm, diameter 23mm, Inv/85/014. Photographs John Bingeman

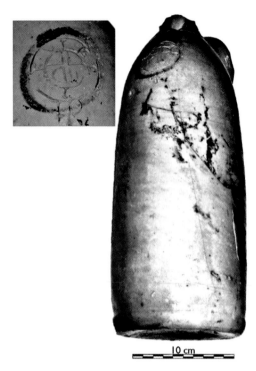

Figure 267. Stoneware 'gin' bottle 263mm high with the letters 'E·X·T·E·R'. around a seal above a 'crown', Inv/85/010. Photographs John Bingeman.

Figure 268. Stoneware jar, no markings standing 9½ inches high (242mm), Inv/80/259. Photograph Christie's South Kensington.

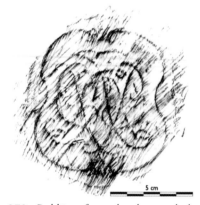

Figure 269. Rim of earthenware vessel. OD 287mm. ID 195mm, Inv/89/105. Photograph John Bingeman

Figure 270. Rubbing from the decorated sherd, max width 110mm, Inv/89/296.

Earthenware

Thirteen pieces from a thick earthenware vessel (all recorded on Inv/89/072) were recovered and thought to be 'Verwood Ware'. One sherd had a decorated scroll (Fig. 270) and the rim is illustrated in Figure 269. Further pieces were recovered from time to time: Inv/89/080, 086, 127, 141, 149, 291, and 293.

An amphora style earthenware jar standing 230mm high is illustrated in Figure 271. Close examination revealed gold specks on its surface suggesting that it may have had some form of gold illumination or writing.

Ceramic handle

A ceramic handle (Fig. 272) was found within an iron concretion. It appears to have had a ferrous rod 3.5mm diameter through its centre, visible at either end and now corroded away. It is likely to have been formed in a mould before being fired. There are indications that the mould was in two halves and that its join marks have been carefully smoothed out. Its exact purpose is uncertain but it might have been the handle for a metal spike. In the bulbous part of the handle is the letter 'A' facing to the left; there was no letter on the reverse side.

Figure 271. Amphora style earthenware jar, height 230mm, Inv/89/045. Photograph John Bingeman.

Figure 272. Ceramic handle, length 93mm, Inv/84/355. Photograph John Bingeman.

Treen

Six square plates were recovered, some of these had a broad arrow on their underside – see Figure 274. Each plate was 12 inches square and had a moulding around the edge known as a 'fiddle'. In Chapter 2 (under Publicity) Alan Rusbridger writes in *The Guardian* newspaper "According to the Oxford English Dictionary people began to have square meals around 1860". Yet the use of square plates goes back far further than *Invincible*'s time. The picture in Figure 273 of the King of Portugal entertaining his future father-in-law, John of Gaunt, shows square plates on the banqueting table during the 14th century.

It seems quite plausible that these artefacts

Figure 273. Square plates in use to entertain John of Gaunt by his future son-in-law, the King of Portugal in 1386.

Figure 274. Square oak plate with scored broad arrow on the reverse, Inv/80/236. Photograph Peter Hales, drawing John R. Terry.

Figure 275. Butter pat(?) partly complete, length 163mm, Inv/89/166. Photograph John Bingeman.

Figure 276. A typical beech bowl, diameter 310mm, Inv/88/337. Photograph John Bingeman.

could have been the origin of the well-known phrases: to eat 'three square meals a day' and 'being on the fiddle' (i.e. when the plate was overfilled)!

A wood artefact (Fig. 275) of uncertain use thought to be a 'butter pat' since it has light grooves and reminded the Licensee of two similar kitchen 'patters' used for making butter balls. It was recovered from the stern section of *Invincible* suggesting its use could have been for the officers' messing.

All but two wooden bowls were lathe turned from beech wood. These were of a fairly standard size around 310mm in diameter (Fig. 276). One had a carved 'HI' on its base. Another (Inv/87/125) had

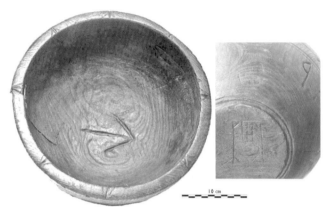

Figure 277. Tudor style elm bowl and underside view, Inv/81/119. Photographs Peter Hales.

Figures 278 and 279. Heavier style elm bowl, diameter 300mm, Inv/86/260.

a whole series of scored marks; inside 'W + T' and 'G + O', and on the outside 'I + T' and 'M + C'.

The first of the two non-standard elm bowls (Fig. 277) was of a heavier construction with 18mm 'walls' within its 300mm diameter. It had a small crack that had been repaired with a whipping threaded through two drilled holes. Some treen experts have suggested that this bowl could be a lot older than the 18th century. Other features were: the eight broad arrows around its rim; a large broad arrow in its base; on its exterior side a carved '9H'; and on the underside base a carving of rectangular boxes reminiscent of a cage used when a criminal was hung, drawn and quartered. It could possibly date back to Tudor times.

When recovered it had a wooden spoon (Inv/81/120), illustrated in Figure 332.

The second of the two heavier style bowls, see Figures 278 and 279, was also made of elm. It had two 'hand-hold flats' on either side, and was scored with a broad arrow on its upturned base.

Ten stave-built, oak buckets were recovered intact, as well as staves from broken-up buckets. They

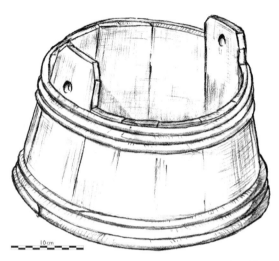

Figure 280. Wooden bucket with original rope handle, Inv/83/046. Photograph Peter Hales.

Figure 281. Wooden bucket sketch by John R. Terry.

Figure 282. Picture courtesy of 'The News, Portsmouth'. Left to right: Cook Denis Gorman (who dived on Invincible), ?, John Broomhead, Peter Hales, Captain Mike Livesay (HMS Invincible's Captain), the Licensee (handing over the bucket), ?, John Terry, and Arthur Mack.

stand 200mm high with a base diameter of 345mm. The banding consists of three hazel hoops top and bottom pinned with an occasional ferrous nail. It is assumed that such buckets were for general-purpose use throughout the ship. A large broad arrow is scratched on the underside of their bases. The bucket in Figure 280 was recovered with the original rope lanyard strung between the two extended staves to provide a handle.

One similar but modified bucket (Inv/85/082) had the hazel bands replaced with two iron bands and a 50mm diameter hole in the base centre. Around the central hole were remains of ferrous concretions suggesting that a ferrous pipe had been attached to make this wooden bucket into some form of funnel.

One of these buckets (Inv/80/216) was presented to HMS *Invincible* on the 6th November 1981 (Fig. 282). This was seen as a suitable gesture from the First *Invincible* to the Sixth *Invincible*. From time to time *Invincible's* divers had joined us to dive on the wreck site.

Stave-built tankards

Details of stave-built tankards are illustrated in Figures 283 to 288.

Seen in Figures 287 and 288, the tankard's lid with letters 'I and R' either side of the anchor, prompted the Licensee to investigate the owner's name. Checking through *Invincible's* Muster List Index[2] for the period 25th December 1756 to 5th March 1758, I could find only one crew member with the initials 'IR'. His name was Isaac Robinson (Ship's Book No. 279), with the notation 'Yeoman Powder Room'. He was discharged to join *Barfleur* on the 30th April 1757. *Invincible's* Muster List shows he received his net wages of £6 18s 4d on the 3rd February 1758 for a period of just over four-months service.

The *Barfleur* had been Captain John Bentley's previous command. When Bentley took command of *Invincible* on the 30th April, he was allowed to bring a certain number of his old crew with him. Isaac Robinson would have been one of those selected to replace them on board *Barfleur*.

We will never know if Isaac Robinson failed to take his tankard with him to *Barfleur* nor, indeed, whether a new 'owner' tried to polish out Isaac's initials.

In the modern world it seems odd that *Invincible's* Muster List for her final commission should have started on 25th December 1756. You would expect Christmas celebrations to be taking place. A hundred years before, Cromwell and his Puritans had suppressed Christmas celebrations and Christmas had become a normal working day. Christmas Day once again became a time of celebration and a public holiday in the early 19th century.

Figure 283. Stave-built tankard before and after conservation. Unlike other tankards, it had no banding but a twine whipping instead; this was replaced during conservation. Height 180mm, Inv/80/239.

Figure 284. The floral patterned lid to Inv/80/239 (Fig. 283). From: Heart of Oak – A Sailors Life in Nelson's Navy by James P. McGuane. © 2002 James P. McGuane. Used by permission of W. W. Norton and Company.

Figure 285. A similar tankard to Fig. 283, but wider, height 167mm. The tankard had narrow hazel/willow(?) banding which disintegrated, Inv/89/312. Photograph John Bingeman.

Figure 286. Tankard base with 'circles', Inv/88/216. Photograph Geoff Lee.

Figure 287. Tankard with 'Anchor' Lid, height 167mm (not all the banding is original), Inv/89/325. Photographs John Bingeman.

Figure 288. 'Anchor' lid of tankard, Inv/89/325. Drawing by John R. Terry.

Figure 289. Bosun's cane made of bamboo 960 × 12mm, Inv/84/095.

A Bosun's cane (Fig. 289) was often referred to as a 'starter' to get a reluctant sailor moving, while the sailors referred to it as the 'Bosun's daughter'. When re-measured in 2007, it had shrunk to 955mm.

A treen object thought to be a crudely hollowed out cup is illustrated in Figure 290. Another artefact (not illustrated) is an oak block of wood 50 × 50 × 23mm high with a central hole diameter 25mm and 15mm deep. It is thought to have been used as a base for a candle – Inv/84/008.

Figure 291 is one of two cone-shaped bamboo baskets. Their use and purpose is not known. The second cone was fragmented (Inv/88/300).

Figure 292 is an oak box with drawer measuring 18 × 8 inches, height 9 inches. When emptied in the Conservation Laboratory it was disappointing to find that it had no artefacts inside.

Three hammock stretchers were recovered. Two in oak (Inv/88/245 and Inv/86/364) and the third in teak (Inv/86/365). Figure 293 was the most ornate of the three recovered with slots for 18 clew lines.

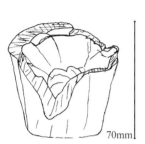

Figure 290. A treen object thought to be a crudely hollowed out cup, Inv/80/96. Drawing Simon Aked.

Figure 291. Cone-shaped bamboo basket, overall length 290mm, Inv/88/291. Photograph Geoff Lee.

Figure 292. Oak box with no lid, Inv/89/154. Photograph John Bingeman.

Figure 293. Oak hammock stretcher, Inv/88/245. Photograph John Bingeman.

Writing kits

A total of twenty-seven whole miniature barrels (Fig. 294) were recovered. For many years we were puzzled about their function. The contents consisted of very fine sand and, at one end, a black gooey substance. This gooey substance was analysed as 97% carbon with iron and a small trace of gallic acid. We now consider that these miniature barrels were 'writing kits', the sand for use as a blotting medium and the black substance the ingredient for ink. Prior to spending over 200 years underwater, the 'black gooey' substance could have been black dry powder or perhaps a powder cake.

After many years of research into the miniature barrels, the only evidence we found to support this hypothesis is a 1764 shop sign. The shop, near St. Giles Church, London, announces the trade of Joseph Pitcher, to be a colourman or oilman. The sign (Fig. 295) depicted a 'Good woman'; namely a beautifully painted lady in a long dress without a head, and, on either side, two barrels resembling our miniature barrels; these were sometimes described as 'pigment barrels'.

A piece of 97mm long cane with a diameter of 10mm (Fig. 296) is thought to have been an early type of an eighteenth century 'pencil'. It had a sharpened burnt point; if you wet the end, it absorbs water and works like a pencil making legible writing.

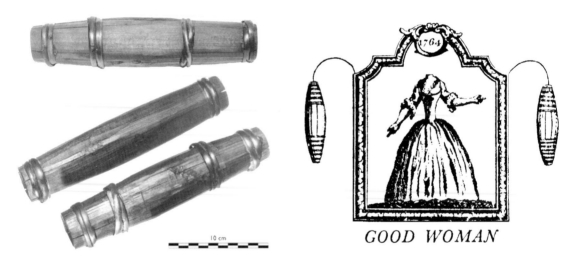

GOOD WOMAN

Figure 294. Top: First miniature barrel recovered, Inv/80/104. There were two styles with either two or four bands. Two bands, Inv/81/145. Four bands, Inv/81/146. Photographs Peter Hales.

Figure 295. The Joseph Pitcher shop sign.[3]

Figure 296. Eighteenth century 'pencil', Inv/87/152. Photograph Geoff Lee.

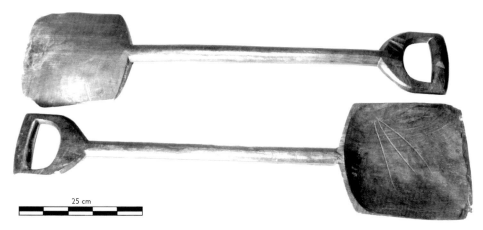

Figure 297. Shod shovels with a scratched broad arrow. Top: Inv/81/090 Bottom: Inv/80/120. Photograph Peter Hales.

Figure 298. Three coal nuggets recovered with the shod shovel found in the coal locker at the stern, Inv/85/038. Photograph John Bingeman.

Shod shovels

Eleven shod shovels (Fig. 297) and various fragments were recovered; they were probably used for shovelling ballast. A metal rim would have protected the blades, but this had now corroded away leaving traces of corrosion as well as small rusty holes from the nails that had held the rim. One shod shovel was found in the coal locker at *Invincible*'s stern – see coal nuggets in Figure 298.

Barrels

During the excavations a significant number of barrel staves were recovered ranging from those used for small spirit casks to staves from 4½ foot high barrels known as 'Butts'. These are recorded among the artefacts listed in the artefact records on the enclosed CD-ROM.

Examples of partly complete spirit barrels are featured in Figures 299, 300 and 301.

Figure 299. Spirit barrel, bottom and cork bungs, height 440mm, end diameter 245mm, Inv/84/297. Photograph J. A. Hewes.

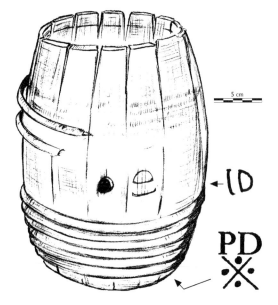

Figure 300. Small spirit barrel, height 12 inches, diameter 8 inches Marked: on side 'ID', and on base 'PD' and 'X with dots'. Banding consisted of: six bottom and four top bands, Inv/80/222. Sketch John Terry.

Figure 301. A partly restored barrel with markings 'ID and X'. Photograph John Bingeman.

Figure 299 is a typical reconstructed spirit barrel with 14 staves. This barrel had various markings: one stave was marked 'WT', and another had figures '1–2–3' both above and below an 'X'. In addition to a cork bung in the barrel's end, one stave had a wooden bung in its centre.

When a barrel was broached, a spout (Fig. 302) was inserted to make pouring of the contents easier.

Cooking

Invincible was fitted with the latest type of cooking range (see Fig. 186) during her refit at Portsmouth which was completed in April 1756. This range was recovered from the wreck in 1758.

When the two cooking cauldrons (Figures 303 and 304) were found near the surface full of artefacts, I concluded that they had been used as convenient containers for recovering smaller items of ship's stores. Why the two had been abandoned when full, is not known.

The larger cauldron measured 36 inches (915mm) diameter and was built-up from four copper-riveted side panels. It contained mainly rigging gear, including the largest fiddle block (Fig. 117).

The other smaller copper cauldron was slightly tapered with two brass handles. Among the artefacts inside were two iron cauldrons (Fig. 305), a carpenter's saw (handle only surviving – Fig. 370), a snatch block (Fig. 107) and numerous other small items. The iron had reacted with the cauldron's copper to cause the severe deterioration as seen in Figure 304.

Figure 302. Bamboo barrel spout, length 187mm, external diameter 28mm. Inv/89/260. From: Heart of Oak – A Sailors Life in Nelson's Navy by James P. McGuane. Copyright © 2002 by James P. McGuane. Used by permission of W. W. Norton and Company.

Figure 303. The larger 36 inch cauldron, height 617mm, diameter 915mm, Inv/86/079. Photograph Peter Hales.

Figure 304. The smaller copper cauldron, height 685mm, Inv/87/045. Photograph Geoff Lee.

Figure 305. Iron cooking pot (Inv/87/055) was inside a similar larger version (Inv/87/054) and these were both recovered in the smaller copper cauldron (Fig. 304). Photograph John Bingeman.

Figure 306. A red brick 228 × 115 × 65mm, Inv/81/216. Photograph John Bingeman.

Figure 307. Sandstone block 150 × 70 × 35mm, Inv/86/347. Photograph Geoff Lee.

Galley bricks

A large number of red bricks (Fig. 306) were recovered, of which thirty-five are in the collection at Chatham Historic Dockyard. It is assumed that they were used to line the hearth in the Ship's Galley.

Holystone

Holystones, made of soft sandstone, were used for scouring decks. Two were recovered within the wreck; the one illustrated (Fig. 307), and the other is at the Royal Naval Museum, Portsmouth Dockyard (Inv/84/007). They were often referred to as 'bibles' as sailors used them while kneeling down. When I was in the Cadet Training ship, HMS *Devonshire* in 1952, we used them to keep the teak decks in pristine condition. A line of us would work our way down the decks scrubbing with these dampened sandstone blocks.

Figure 308. Grindstone wheel, Inv/87/093 and Mortar bowl, Inv/86/337. Photographs Peter Hales.

Figures 309 and 310. Square: 36 × 36 × 13mm, Inv/89/246. round: diameter 28mm, 5mm thick, Inv/87/153. Photographs John Bingeman.

Stone artefacts

We recovered three grindstone wheels made of sandstone. The first grindstone wheel (Inv/86/317) had worn down to 485mm (19 inches) diameter. The second (Fig. 308) had a diameter of 522mm (20½ inches). The third (Inv/89/099) was only one quarter complete. The drive hole in the centre of each wheel was 3 inches square and their width was 101/105mm (4 inches).

Another sandstone artefact was a mortar bowl (Inv/86/337) that was far from complete (Fig. 308).

Games

During the eleven years of excavation a number of gaming pieces were recovered. Figures 309 and 310 are typical examples, both made from pine wood. A gaming board with 8 × 8 squares could have been a chess or draughts board – Figure 311.

'Fox and Geese', an old traditional game going back many hundreds of years, is played on a board similar to Figure 312 recovered from *Invincible*. It is normally played with a red or black draught representing the fox, and fifteen white draughts representing the geese. The fox starts in the middle of the board and the geese occupy all 6 squares of one arm of the cross plus the whole first adjacent row. The geese cannot capture the fox but aim, through the benefit of numbers, to hem the fox in so that he cannot move. The objective of the fox is to capture geese until it becomes impossible for them to trap him.

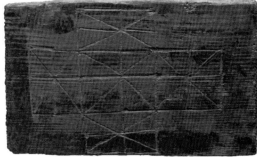

Figure 311. Gaming board with 8 × 8 squares, Inv/85/068. Photograph Peter Hales.

Figure 312. The 'Fox and Geese' pine games board – 200 × 120 × 12mm, Inv/86/184. From: Heart of Oak – A Sailors Life in Nelson's Navy *by James P. McGuane. © 2002 James P. McGuane. Used by permission of W. W. Norton and Company.*

Leather

Seven hides were recovered from within the Forward Magazine. It looked as if they were being used as a form of covering possibly for protection against the risk of fire. Some were physically joined to the powder barrels by the reaction of the copper bands becoming a copper oxide concretion. The hide reference numbers are:

> Inv/84/191
> Inv/86/317 and 329
> Inv/87/046, 073, 093, and 138

One leather fragment Figure 313 had a manufacturer or Government mark of the French 'Fleur-de-Lis' with 'CUIRS' directly underneath, and around the outside in a circle at the top 'CHGONT' and at 6 o'clock 'GTO'. It may have been a legacy from when *Invincible* belonged to the French Navy.

Various strips of leather with stitch holes were recovered and identified as rope sheathing to prevent wear – see Figure 314. The practice has been referred to as 'parcelling' (See Chapter 4, Fig. 145).

Leather sheathing reference numbers:
> Inv/86/104, 208, 262, 263, 264, and 278 to 285 inclusive
> Inv/89/158 and 168

A one-metre length of leather pipe (Inv/80/013), dark brown in colour, was recovered from the surface of the seabed on the 10th April 1980. The pipe was constructed by rolling leather together so that it overlapped, and then securing the overlapping with copper rivets. From memory, the pipe diameter was approximately 2 inches (50mm).

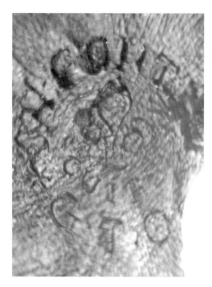

Figure 313. Fragment of leather with stamp mark.

Figure 314. Pieces of leather thought to have been used for 'parcelling'. Top: Inv/89/158, bottom: Inv/uncertain. Photograph John Bingeman.

Figure 315. A typical 18th century leather shoe of welt construction with the uppers partially cut away. Length 230mm.

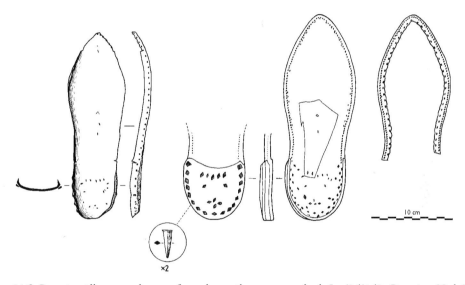

Figure 316. Drawing illustrates the use of wooden nails to secure a heel, Inv/84/148. Drawing Nick Evans.

Shoes

During the ten years of the site's excavation, roughly 200 shoes were recovered, many incomplete, see Figure 315 as a typical example. These included a child's shoe and ladies shoes with semi-high heels. Thirty-one full-sized drawings were made on permatrace to illustrate the various types of shoes. See Figures 316, 317 and 318 for representative examples of these drawings.

Many of the shoes recovered had a 'DC' mark, standing for 'Deceased's Clothing' – see Figure 317. It was, and still is, the practice to auction a man's effects to raise funds for the widow. Often prices paid are far in excess of the items' value as a gesture of goodwill. The practice is to stamp effects sold in this way with 'DC' to show that they are not stolen.

Other marks on shoe soles were initials 'IA' and circular marks usually in twos (diameter 6mm) whose significance is not known.

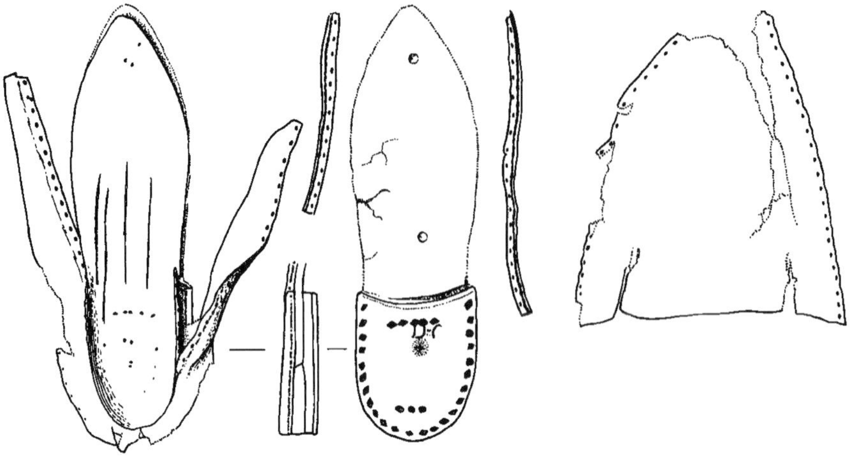

Figure 317. A typical shoe, note the 'DC' stamp on the heel, Inv/85/044. Drawing Nick Evans.

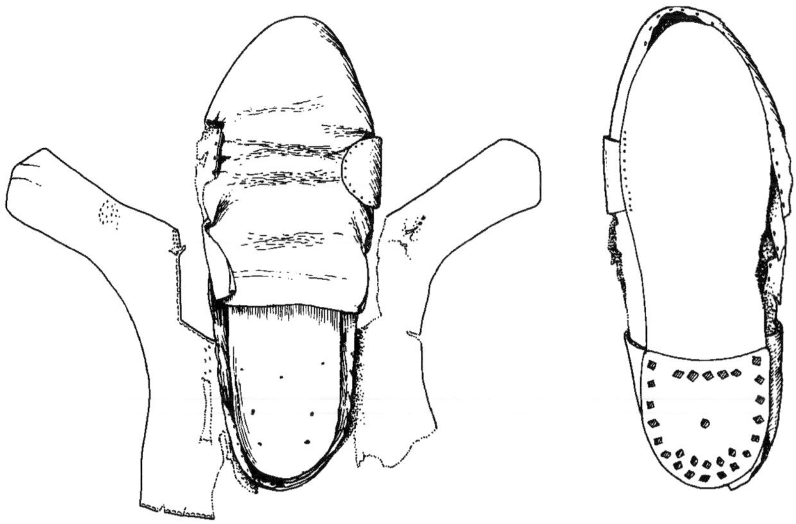

Figure 318. Another typical shoe drawing, Inv/86/261. Drawing Nick Evans.

A shoe that could have belonged to a lady (Fig. 319) makes us wonder if women and children were onboard *Invincible* since it is known that from time to time families took passage in naval ships. We also know that part of the Fleet going to Louisbourg was programmed to stop at Gibraltar before crossing the Atlantic.

A child's shoe (Fig. 320) raises an interesting question. Why should a shoe suitable for a five or six year old be found within the hull of *Invincible*? Could it have been the child of a person taking passage, or a youngster learning the trade as a seaman? It was known that youngsters learnt their trade as 'Topmen' at a very young age. This enabled them to achieve a remarkable sense of balance, conquering any fear of falling. Passengers or children were not listed on the Ship's Muster List.

A second complete child's shoe (Inv/86/060) length 8⅜ inches (214mm), had been tied with lace

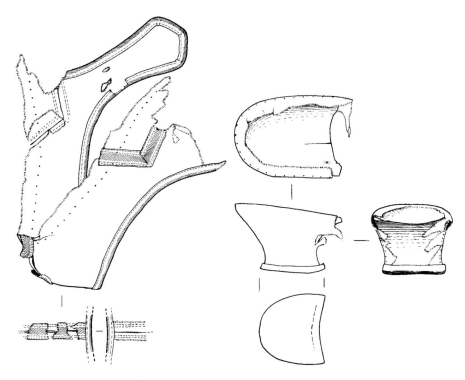

Figure 319. A lady's shoe? Inv/80/276. Drawing Nick Evans.

10 cm

Figure 320. A child's shoe – length of inner sole 6⅞ inches (170mm), Inv/86/059.

and had a broad arrow mark. Inside it had toe marks showing that the shoe had been worn on either foot alternately.

Wearing shoes alternately on either foot seems to have been common practice, presumably to lengthen the life of the shoe. Soldiers of the period are known to have been ordered to do this, and double 'big toe' marks were found on many of the 200 shoes recovered.

A patten (Fig. 321) was a type of over-shoe, pre-dating galoshes, to protect the wearer's shoes in

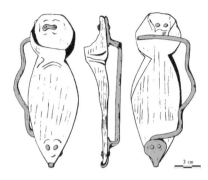

Figure 321. A patten with straps; the iron 'base' and nails are missing, Inv/86/218. Photograph Peter Hales.

Figure 322. A similar patten with part of the iron base missing.[4]

Figure 323. Cobbler's lasts. Left/right: lengths 245 and 220mm, Inv/85/063 and Inv/86/352. Photographs Peter Hales.

muddy conditions. Only half a pair was found with its iron 'base' corroded away. The missing ferrous base is illustrated in Figure 322.

A pair of pattens such as these are among the period clothing display at Jane Austen's Hampshire home at Chawton where she wrote the majority of her world famous novels.

Two wooden shoe formers or cobbler's lasts (Fig. 323) were recovered approximately 10 metres apart on consecutive years. A similar last appeared in the *Swift* report.[5] The *Swift* was a sloop built in 1763 and was part of the small British Fleet based in the Falkland Islands. She struck rocks and sank off Patagonia, southern Argentina in 1770, when taking shelter whilst carrying out survey work.

Buckles

A whole variety of buckles were recovered and some of these are illustrated in Figures 324 to 329.

The central pin in most buckles was ferrous and had corroded away. The ornate surrounds were detached from the brass centres and even with delicate excavations the two were not always associated together. Fortunately in the case of Figure 324, the two parts were kept together and the ferrous central pin could be replaced during conservation.

During the course of excavations, pieces of buckles illustrated in Figure 329 were recovered from the stern area of *Invincible*. They would have originated from the clothing worn by the officer class.

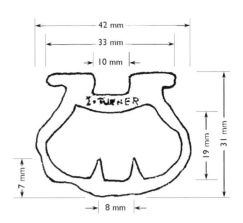

Figure 324. While incomplete, an impressive shoe buckle manufactured by 'Turner'. Other buckles had 'I Turner', Inv/89/314. From: Heart of Oak – A Sailors Life in Nelson's Navy by James P. McGuane. © 2002 James P. McGuane. Used by permission of W. W. Norton and Company.

Figure 325. Buckle centre with 'I·Turner', Inv/80/250. Drawing John Broomhead.

Figures 326 and 327. Left: pewter shoe buckle with brass centre, Inv/86/331. Right: ornate pewter buckle, Inv/80/178. Photographs Peter Hales.

Figure 328. Brass ornate buckle, Inv/89/317. From: Heart of Oak – A Sailors Life in Nelson's Navy by James P. McGuane. © 2002 James P. McGuane. Used by permission of W. W. Norton and Company.

Figure 329. Top row: left Inv/89/320, centre Inv/ NK, right Inv/89/322. Identification numbers of the remainder are uncertain. Photograph John Bingeman.

Spoons

These are illustrated in Figures 330 to 338.

When searching *Invincible*'s Muster List[6] to identify the owner of the spoon in Figure 335, ten members of the Ship's Company were found to have the initials 'TH'. The most likely person is Thomas Hilliard who joined as Lieutenant Robert Curry's steward. On his final entry on the Muster List, he is shown as a Captain's steward and was onboard at the time of *Invincible*'s stranding. Hilliard's Ship's Book numbers are: 498, 598 and 856 – each time he rejoined *Invincible*, he was given a new number. Lieutenant Curry was 6th Lieutenant when he joined on the 4th January 1757 and became 3rd Lieutenant on 11th July 1757. Curry's log[7] from the 19th and 23rd of February 1758, has one of the best descriptions of the disaster.

The engraving in the spoon bowl (Fig. 338) reminds us of a 'capstan' being manned by both marines and sailors. The drawing Figure 339 shows 72 men on the capstan bars and another 12 on the outer rope. While details of *Invincible*'s capstan are not known precisely, capstans can be manned by up to 96 men on each tier of a double capstan. *Invincible*'s 700 complement included 96 marines and four marine officers.

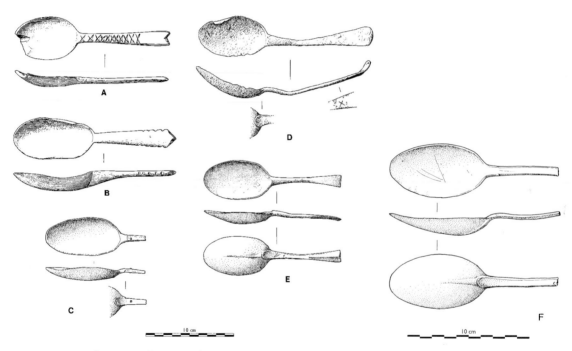

Figure 330. A and B are wood, C, D and E are pewter. A = Inv/81/120, B = Inv/83/197a, C = Inv/83/233, D = Inv/83/198, and E = Inv/83/197b. Drawing Nick Evans 1985.

Figure 331. Pewter spoon with broad arrow, Inv/83/232. Drawing Nick Evans.

Figure 332. Treen spoon (Inv/81/120) found in elm bowl (Fig. 277). Photograph Peter Hales.

Figure 333. Treen spoon, wood uncertain, Inv/83/197a. Photograph John Bingeman.

Figure 334. A particularly fine wooden table spoon made from sycamore, length 227mm, Inv/86/307. Photograph J. A. Hewes.

Figure 335. Pewter spoon top and bottom, 'LONDON and crown' pewter mark, 'K' in the bowl and 'TH' on the handle underside, Inv/86/114. Photographs Geoff Lee.

Figure 336. Pewter 18th century spoon, top and bottom, Inv/89/226. Photographs John Bingeman

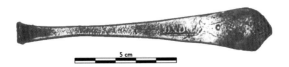

Figure 337. Pewter spoon handle with a LONDON touch mark, and 'T' and 'B' underneath two 'crown' type motifs, Inv/88/293. Photograph John Bingeman.

Figure 338. Pewter spoon bowl with a 'capstan' engraving, Inv/87/047. Photograph John Ambler, Royal Marines Museum, Portsmouth.

Figure 339. An 18th century engraving of a capstan crew. The sailors are on the left and the marines on the right.

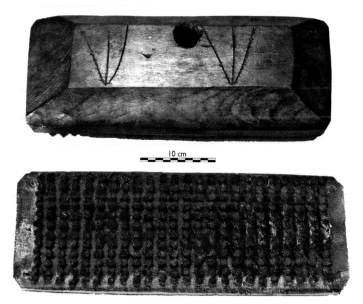

10 cm

Figure 340. Beech deck brushes. Overall size: 290 × 133 × 90mm high. Top: Inv/81/142; bottom: Inv/81/118. Photograph Peter Hales.

Brushes

Around a dozen deck 'bumper' brushes were recovered with two types of bristles. Figure 340 has badger bristle hair secured at the back with copper wire. Similar brushes were found with softer hair, the majority of which had deteriorated.

These deck brushes were invariably recovered in two halves because they relied on six small ferrous nails to hold them together, and these had been destroyed by corrosion. The three nail head stains can be seen in the lower half of Figure 340 at either end.

Figure 341 shows the underside of a bristle plate where copper wire lacing secures the bristles. The corrosion stains on the right are from the iron nails that secured the bristle plate to the main brush body.

Various other brushes are illustrated in Figures 342 to 346.

Around 160 of the 180 besom brushes (Fig. 346) listed on the ship's manifest have been recovered. They were used for 'breaming', the practice of burning off the growth when careening. This was an essential hull cleaning task despite the risk of fire since even slight growth would slow a ship down. The besom brushes were found closely packed together in a store just aft of the Gunner's Store on the Ship's port side.

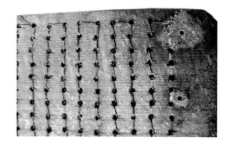

Figure 341. Bristle plate showing copper wiring. Photograph John Broomhead.

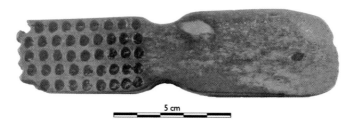

Figure 342. A bone combined brush and shoe horn, Inv/88/315. Photograph John Bingeman.

Figure 343. Paint brush, and head enlarged, length 350mm, Inv/87/009. Photographs: top: John Bingeman, bottom from: Heart of Oak – A Sailors Life in Nelson's Navy *by James P. McGuane. © 2002 James P. McGuane. Used by permission of W. W. Norton and Company.*

Figures 344 and 345. Oak backed hand brushes. Left: length 205mm, Inv/80/301. Right: length 140mm, Inv/86/005. Photographs Geoff Lee.

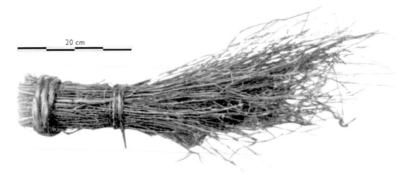

Figure 346. Besom brush length 670mm, Inv/81/127. Photograph Peter Hales.

Figure 347. One of two lead ingots weighing 8lbs, Inv/81/028. Photograph John Bingeman.

Lead artefacts

A whole variety of lead artefacts have been recovered. These are illustrated in Figures 347 to 358.

Not illustrated were a lead pipe with flange 700 x 80mm (Inv/80/012) and a lead pipe approximately 2 metres long with an outside diameter of 32mm (Inv/89/276).

The use of the lead lining (Fig. 352) is uncertain. Its most likely purpose was to line a sink or drawer. Figure 353 is part of a lead drain flange with traces of an oblong pipe that had been fused to its central hole. The flange had 16 securing nail holes, and a scratched broad arrow.

Figure 348. Lead trough with drain pipe, Inv/89/306. Photographs John Bingeman.

Figure 349. A weighted 'shoe' suitable for a wooden stave with three securing holes, base diameter 5cm, Inv/83/187. Photograph Geoff Lee.

Figure 350. Inv/81/212A and Inv/NK. Two similar lead brackets – the right-hand bracket has the remains of what may have been a broom handle stump. Photographs John Bingeman.

Figure 351. Lead strainer 120 × 124mm with 8 securing nail holes, Inv/80/133. From: Heart of Oak – A Sailors Life in Nelson's Navy *by James P. McGuane. © 2002 James P. McGuane. Used by permission of W. W. Norton and Company.*

Figure 352. Base measured approximately 60 × 40cm, Inv/88/137. Photograph John Bingeman.

Figure 353. Lead square flange, 142 × 203 × 9mm, Inv/90/027. Photograph John Bingeman.

Figure 354. Lead moon shaped object, perhaps an off-cut. Thickness 3mm, outside diameter 180mm, Inv/90/28. Photograph John Bingeman.

Figure 355. Brass weights. Left: diameter 112mm, height 22mm, Inv/89/098. Centre: diameter 62mm, height 12mm, Inv/89/119. Right: height 153mm, Inv/89/097.

Figure 356. Lead weights. Top right: Inv/89/104, height 81mm, dia. 95mm. Far left: Inv/89/110 lead height 40mm, dia. 69mm.

Figure 357. Lead and brass weight, height 100mm, base diameter 72mm. The brass covering is missing in the centre showing three of the lead discs, weight 7lb, Inv/89/106. Photograph John Bingeman.

Weights

Weights of various shapes and sizes were recovered from *Invincible*'s stern area – Figures 355 to 357. Their material varied from brass or bronze to lead, and a mix using a brass shell with lead discs inside. One lead weight, Inv/89/981, height 85mm, diameter 68mm, had two guild marks: a 'woman with scales and crown', and a 'dagger mark'.

Figure 357 weight was built up of ten lead discs, average thickness 10mm, covered by a thin layer

Figure 358. Unconserved 'tube' weight with rope remains. Length 41mm, diameters: internal 17mm, external 25/27mm, Inv/92/001. Photograph John Bingeman.

of brass. On the top, there were traces of a corroded ferrous hook, and the figures '368'. It is similar to a weight from a small grandfather clock.

Many of these tube weights (Fig. 358) were found a metre below the surface within the coherent hull structure. What was their purpose? There are two possible explanations: fishing nets may have been carried onboard, or late-18th century fishermen may have fouled their nets on *Invincible*'s timbers. The rope remains within the tube are old so it does seem likely that the weights could belong to the 18th century.

I recall that in the 1960s, all Royal Naval ships carried a seine net as part of their stores' outfit. Perhaps it was the same in the 18th century?

Metal artefacts

Besides the barrel tap in Figure 359, a second brass/bronze tap thought to have come from a 'silver' plated urn was recovered – Inv/89/241.

In Figure 360, the Licensee was surprised to find that an 18th century brass escutcheon's closing plate should be a hollow casting. It is secured to the backplate by a course threaded screw.

One of three brass mortice door locks with all their ferrous insides corroded away is illustrated in Figure 361.

A copper tube (Fig. 363) was thought to be part of a rum barrel pump similar to those used by the Royal Navy up to 1970 when the issue of rum was discontinued. Its construction was interesting. The copper sheet had been perfectly rolled together, butt jointed with square mortises and sealed with solder.

Figure 359. Barrel tap (91mm long), Inv/89/107. Photograph Brandon Mason.

Two small brass padlocks of similar design were recovered (Fig. 362). Both had lost their ferrous hasps. The padlock (Inv/81/020) not illustrated measured 25 × 24 × 6mm.

The only medical artefact found was this rather damaged pewter syringe. After its removal from a concretion containing other items, Figure 364 shows it in pieces revealing its plunger with the remains of a leather piston seal. Illustrated at Figure 365 is a similar syringe recovered from 'The Needles' wreck site. This was a mixed scattered site so the syringe could easily have been an artefact from *Assurance*

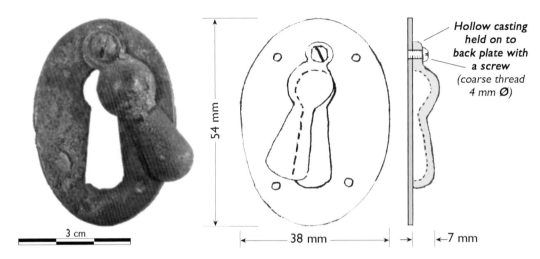

Hollow casting
held on to
back plate with
a screw
(coarse thread
4 mm Ø)

54 mm

38 mm

7 mm

3 cm

Figure 360. Brass escutcheon, Inv/82/014. Photograph and drawing John Broomhead.

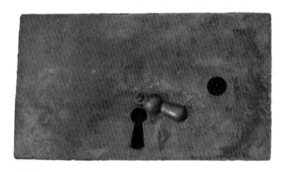

Figure 361. Brass mortice door lock, its ferrous inside had corroded away, measurements 200 × 115 × 28mm. Inv/82/007. From: Heart of Oak – A Sailors Life in Nelson's Navy *by James P. McGuane. © 2002 James P. McGuane. Used by permission of W. W. Norton and Company.*

Figure 362. The larger of the two brass padlocks, 32 × 30 × 8mm, Inv/82/016. Photograph Brandon Mason.

25 cm

Figure 363. Copper tube: length 973mm, diameter of 49mm, Inv/89/255.

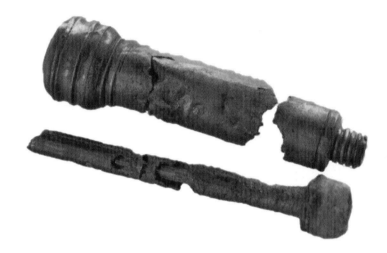

Figure 364. Pewter syringe recovered from within a concretion, Inv/89/327. From: Heart of Oak – A Sailors Life in Nelson's Navy *by James P. McGuane. © 2002 James P. McGuane. Used by permission of W. W. Norton and Company.*

Figure 365. For comparison, a similar syringe from 'The Needles' wreck site, circa either 1753 or 1811, body length 71mm. Photograph John Bingeman.

(1753) or *Pomone* (1811). The *Invincible* (1758) syringe appears to be a more advanced design with a threaded nozzle compared to 'The Needles' site's syringe with a simple cone.

Miscellaneous artefacts

Similar to Figure 366 were floral-decorated grey salt-glazed chamber-pots with cobalt blue motifs found while excavating Oyster Street, Old Portsmouth in 1968–71.[8] These chamber-pots were manufactured in the Westerwald Region of Germany.

A flea comb was recovered in mint condition (Fig. 367).

Figure 368 is one of four wig curlers recovered. Two (Inv/83/029 and Inv/84/015) had the marks 'W.B' cast into each end. In addition, Inv/84/015 had a small 'anchor' mark between the W and B at either end. Figure 368 and Inv/83/209 had no end marks.

Besides the tool parts in Figures 369 and 370, various other tool parts were recovered. A wooden wedge from a plane measuring 65 × 115mm (Inv/87/034) was a typical example. Others were: three

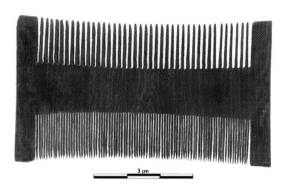

Figure 366. Grey salt-glazed stoneware chamber-pot, Inv/89/177. Photograph John Ambler, Royal Marines Museum, Portsmouth.

Figure 367. Flea comb, Inv/90/067. Photograph John Bingeman.

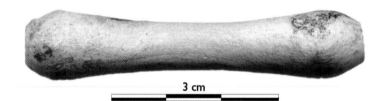

Figure 368. Wig curler, Inv/89/217. Photograph John Bingeman.

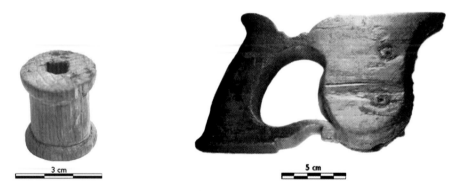

Figures 369 and 370. Left: thought to be part of a hand drill, Inv/85/048. Right: saw handle, blade had corroded away, Inv/87/050. Photographs Peter Hales (left), John Bingeman (right).

wooden mallets (Inv/87/024 and 155, and Inv/89/279; and a sledge hammer handle (Inv/87/074), length 30 inches (764mm) with stains from its corroded head.

The metal disc within this sailmaker's palm (Fig. 371) has corroded away. Its position can be clearly seen in the centre of the right-hand side of the illustration, where, after conservation, the palm still contains small pieces of iron oxide among the ferrous stains. A modern sailmakers' palm in Figure 372 makes a nice comparison.

Figure 371. Sailmakers' palm front and back, diameter 100mm, Inv/86/115. Photograph Geoff Lee.

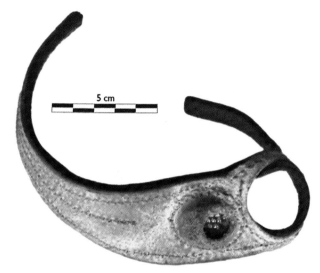

Figure 372. A modern sailmakers' palm for comparison, the basic design has not changed over centuries. Photograph John Bingeman.

Notes

1. Dr Brian A. Plunkett's Portsmouth Polytechnic letter reporting findings dated 7th February 1989.
2. NA ADM 32/96
3. Heal, Sir A., 1947, *The Signboards of old London shops*. Batesford, London.
4. Fox, R. and Barton, K. J., *Excavations at Oyster Street, Portsmouth, Hampshire, 1968–71*. Post-Medieval Archaeology 20 (1986), 31–255.
5. D. Elkin *et al.*, *Archaeological Research on HMS Swift: lost off Patagonia, 1770*, IJNA (2007) 36.1, 49, fig. 17.
6. NA ADM 32/96
7. NMM ADM/L/J/87
8. Fox, R. and Barton, K. J., *Excavations at Oyster Street, Portsmouth, Hampshire, 1968–71*. Post-Medieval Archaeology 20 (1986), 31–255.

7. Conclusion

It has been a great privilege to have been the Licensee of this important historic wreck site. As an enthusiastic amateur nautical archaeologist, my hope is that I have fulfilled my responsibilities to an acceptable standard. It has been a long struggle to compile this book covering my eleven years of excavations, and eighteen more years of research and writing.

How fortunate I have been to have had such a prestigious historical wreck site to work on. It has been a fascinating experience as I believe this book will show.

I can pay this magnificent ship, that became such an integral part of my life, the 74-gun *Invincible*, no better tribute than to include the Admiralty Office manuscript letter instructing the building of the *Valiant* and *Triumph* to her exact scantlings. The letter (Fig. 373) is signed by three Admirals including the Honourable Edward Boscawen, who knew *Invincible* intimately; she had served as his Flagship in 1756 while blockading the French in their home ports. These identical sister ships, particularly *Triumph*, continued to justify the high regard that Captains had for '74's based on (dare we say it) Morineau's French design.

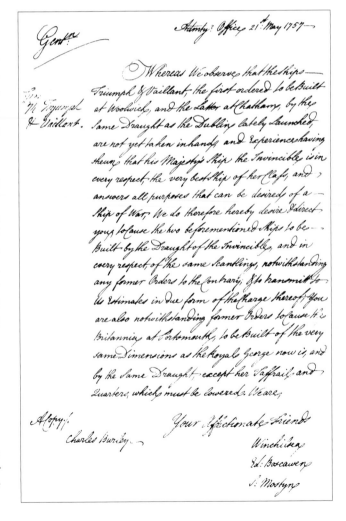

Figure 373. The famous letter saying: 'Invincible *is in every respect, the very best Ship of her Class, and answers all purposes that can be desired of a Ship of War.'*

Appendix A: Record of Repairs and Deck Plans

by David White

3.5.47   *L'Invincible*, French ship of 74 guns and 700 men, Capt. Grout de St Georges, taken by Vice Admiral Lord Anson's squadron off Cape Finisterre, 1¾°E 24 leagues.

19.5.47   Arrived Portsmouth

20.5.47   Admiralty Order to survey her at Portsmouth – estimated 2 years old.

Length on gundeck	–	171ft 3in
Length on keel for tonnage	–	143ft 6in
Breadth extreme	–	48ft 11in
Depth in hold	–	21ft 3in
Tonnage	–	1826

One anchor of each of the following weights:
60¼ cwt, 60 cwt, 56¼ cwt, 17¾ cwt, 16¼ cwt

One cable of each of the following sizes:
24, 23, 22½, 22 inches (circumference)

19.8.47   The Board of Admiralty agreed to pay £13 per ton for the hull masts and yards
(1826 tons at £13 = £23,738)

21.8.47   Admiralty Order to register her by the name of INVINCIBLE and to fit her for sea.

22.8.47   Admiralty Order to fit her for a flagship

12.1.48   Admiralty Order to cause her to be manned with 650 men and established with the guns undermentioned – viz:

28 in number – 32-pounders
30 in number – 18-pounders
<u>16</u> in number – 9-pounders
<u>74 guns</u>

3.2.48	Grounded or careened, graved and trimmed	)))	(((	Hull &c	£3400 17s 6d
4.2.48	Launched	))	Fitted ((	Rigging and stores &c	<u>£9448 10s 11d</u>
20.2.48	Sailed	)	(	Total	<u>£12,849 8s 5d</u>
22.3.48	King's Order in Council and –				

| 2.4.48 | Admiralty Order. Invincible of 74 guns to have 700 men and 5 lieutenants and a 6th Lieutenant if a flag ship; and all other French Prizes of like magnitude and force, as otherwise his Majesty's Ships of guns when reduced to 74 gun ships, to be allowed the same number of men and lieutenants. |

13.7.48   Arrived Portsmouth

22.11.48   Admiralty Order and –

5.12.48   Navy Board Warrant to reduce her to a Guardship of 140 men.

20.6.49	Grounded or careened)		(Hull &c	£745 7s 6d)
	and graved)		(Rigging and stores &c	£1032 8s 3d
21.6.49	Launched)		(Total	£1777 15s 9d

26.2.50	Grounded or careened)		(Hull &c	£239 5s 9d)
	and graved)		(	
	)	Refitted	(Rigging and stores &c	£273 13s 5d
27.2.50	Launched)		(Total	£512 19s 2d

14.2.51	Grounded or careened)		(Hull &c	£653 6s 9d
	and graved)		(	
	)	Refitted	(Rigging and stores &c	£721 11s 1d
15.2.51	Launched)		(Total	£1374 17s 10d

6.2.52	Docked and graved)		(Hull &c	£572 11s 5d
	)		(	
8.2.52	Launched)	Refitted	(Rigging and stores &c	£5083 18s 11d
	)		(	
1.4.52	Sailed)		(Total	£5656 10s 4d

27.6.52   Arrived Portsmouth

27.1.53   Letter from the Portsmouth Officers giving an account of some defects discovered from which they apprehend the ship to be in a bad condition. (To the Navy Board).

31.1.53   Copy of the above letter sent to the Admiralty for their Lordships information and direction.

1.2.53   Admiralty Order to dock and repair her as soon as a dock can be spared, and to carry on her repairs in preference to any other work.

30.8.53   Docked

20.11.53   Surveyed and found to require a great repair. Estimated £26,000 for the hull and 24 months time.

24.11.53   Copy of the survey sent to the Admiralty for their Lordship's information

28.11.53	Letter from Mr Cleveland to re-survey her in conjunction with the assistant to the Surveyor of the Navy and the Master Shipwright of Deptford.
8.12.53	Re-surveyed and proposed to repair her. Estimate for the hull £26,000 and 18 months time.
10.12.53	Copy of survey sent to the Admiralty.
13.12.53	Admiralty Order to repair her.
28.11.55	Admiralty Order to fit her for a flagship.
17.12.55	Admiralty Order to carry 24 pounders on the upper deck instead of 18 pounders.

1.56	Graved	)	Great Repair	(Hull &c	£25,233 2s 8d
		)	and Fitted	(	
		)		(Rigging, stores &c	£4,559 12s 1d
17.1.56	Launched	)	Fitted with an	(Total	£29,792 14s 9d
		)	Iron Fire	(	
		)	Hearth and a	(	
		)	copper double	(	
		)	kettle	(	
20.3.56	Sailed	)			
11.2.57	Arrived Portsmouth				
21.2.57	Docked, graved	)		(	
	and trimmed	)		(	
10.3.57	Launched	)	Refitted	(	
		)		(	
20.4.57	Sailed	)			
9.11.57	Arrived Portsmouth	)		(	
		)		(	
27.11.57	Docked, graved	)		(Hull &c	£1876 16s 3d
	and trimmed	)		(Rigging, stores &c	£3799 13s 8d
28.11.57	Launched	)	Refitted	(Total	£5676 9s 11d
		)		(	
24.12.57	Sailed	)			

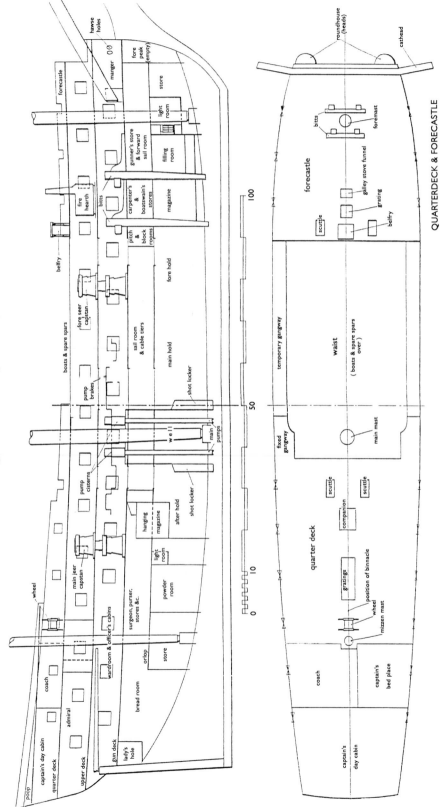

INVINCIBLE 74 guns

Probable arrangement after the Great Repair of the early 1750's

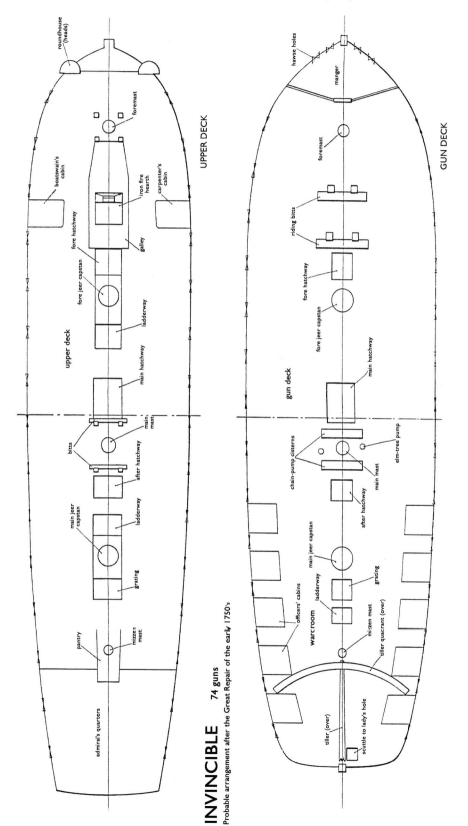

INVINCIBLE 74 guns
Probable arrangement after the Great Repair of the early 1750's

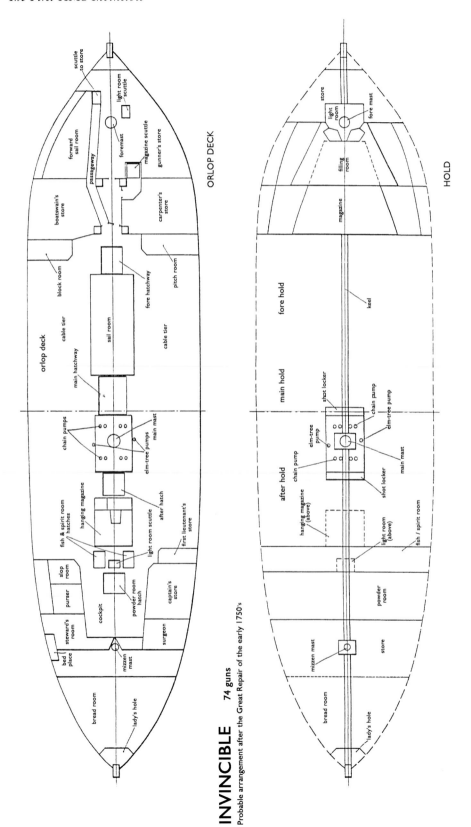

INVINCIBLE 74 guns
Probable arrangement after the Great Repair of the early 1750's

Appendix B: The Dating of Military Buttons

By the Licensee and Arthur T. Mack

First published in the *International Journal of Nautical Archaeology* in 1997.

Introduction

In 1758, the 74-gun ship of the line *Invincible* sank in the Solent when about to carry army personnel to Canada and elsewhere. Research over the last 16 years into buttons found in the wreck establish that numbered military buttons were in regular use prior to 1767, the year most military historians believe they were first introduced. W. Y. Carman, former Deputy Director of the National Army Museum and considered a top living authority on uniforms, when referring to the *Invincible* wreck, wrote:

> 'If actually of 1758 period then many known sources would be wrong and it would be electrifying.'

This paper presents the evidence of numbered buttons from the *Invincible* historic wreck-site together with evidence from four independent sources elsewhere. While evidence from one or two sources might be considered inconclusive, that from five separate sources can no longer be discounted.

Source 1 – *Invincible*

Buttons from the 6th, 13th, 14th, 24th, 30th, 39th, 43rd, 57th, 59th and 64th Regiments of Foot and other military buttons were recovered from the wreck of the Royal Navy's first *Invincible* wrecked in the East Solent on Sunday, 19 February 1758 (Bingeman 1985: 206). The wreck was re-discovered in 1979 by Arthur Mack and was excavated between 1981 and 1990 under a Government licence held by John Bingeman. After the vessel went aground, she fell over onto the port side beam-ends and the hull sank into the seabed to a depth of 3m. The structure above the seabed broke off and can be found scattered to the northeast. Some of the buttons were found close to the surface, others buried up to 2m. Suggestions that so many buttons could have been associated with the wreck at a later date are discounted. Details of the *Invincible* buttons are listed in Appendix A Annex A and in Figures 1 and 2.

Source 2 – Louisbourg 1745 siege lines

A single 65th Regiment of Foot button (Fig. 3) was among the 5 million artefacts recovered by Parks Canada during the recent excavation of the 1745 siege lines around the Fortress of Louisbourg. The button was dated by the Canadian authorities as: 'after 1784 and before 1850', with no explanation as to how the button came to be in the context of the 1745 artefacts. The fortress was razed to the

Figure 1. Buttons recovered from Invincible (1758). Descriptions are listed at the end of this paper. Photos: Peter Hales and Tony Cullen.

ground by British mining engineers in 1760 and the area remained undisturbed until the recent excavation. However, it is known that the 65th (and 66th) Regiments were raised from New Englanders in 1744 by Colonels William Shirley and William Pepperell and that their uniforms, which would have included buttons for the officers' uniforms, were supplied from England. Commodore Peter Warren, Commander in Chief North America, embarked Shirley and Pepperell's regiments as an expedition to attack Louisbourg. Troops were landed with ordnance to lay siege and after skirmishes and bombardments, the French capitulated.

The most likely source of the 65th button was one of Shirley's officers during the 1745 siege. Further, the Louisbourg 65th button has a completely different style of *65* from buttons shown by Parkyn when the Regiment was re-raised in 1758 and subsequently had their own buttons (Parkyn 1956: 279).

Figure 2. Buttons recovered from Invincible (1758). Descriptions are listed at the end of this paper. Photos: Peter Hales and Tony Cullen.

Source 3 – Crown Point, New York State

At the Light Infantry Redoubt, Crown Point State Historic Site, two numbered pewter regimental buttons were excavated in 1963 with the numbers *L* and *51* (Fig. 4).

The 65th and 66th were disbanded after the return of the Fortress of Louisbourg to the French under the Treaty of Aix-la-Chapelle in 1748. Peace did not last long with an increasing number of Anglo-French disputes in North America. In 1754 the same colonels, William Shirley, and now Sir William Pepperell, were approved to raise two new line regiments numbered 50th and 51st.

Confirmation that the uniforms were received from England comes from Sergeant James Grey, who wrote in July 1755 that he had received 'two Holland shirts … two pairs of shoes and two pairs of worsted stockings; a good silver laced hat (the lace I could sell for four dollars); and my clothes in as fine scarlet broadcloth as you ever did see.' (Parkman 1899: II, 6)

The two regiments had only a brief existence. While garrisoning Oswego in August 1756, the French forced the provisionals to surrender and over a thousand officers and men where shipped back to France for exchange. The regiments were formally disbanded on 7 March 1757.

Both the *L* and *51* buttons found at Crown Point were different in style from that shown in Parkyn (1956: 243–50). The English fort at Crown Point was used as a base on Lake Champlain during the Anglo-French and Indian wars.

Source 4 – Publications dated 1757

General Richard Kane's analyses of 'every Battle won or lost, from 1689 to 1712' are included by 'A Gentleman of the Army' in a book entitled *A System of Camp Discipline* published in London in 1757 for the sum of seven shillings and sixpence (Anon. 1757). On page 47 it refers to 'white buttons and L' when describing the uniforms of the 50th and 51st regiments. This confirms that numbered buttons were in circulation ten years before they were officially introduced. The description 'L' identifies the button found at Crown Point; later regimental 50th buttons all bore '50' and there is no record of the Roman numeral 'L' being used. 'White buttons' refers to pewter being used for button making.

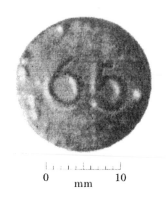

Figure 3. 65th Regiment of Foot button recovered at the Fortress of Louisbourg. Diameter 18mm. Photo: John Bingeman.

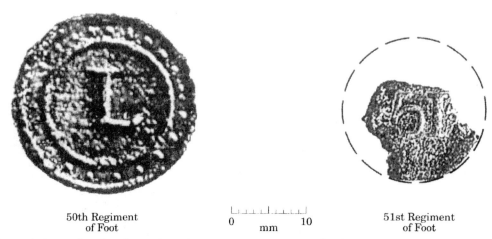

50th Regiment of Foot   51st Regiment of Foot

Figure 4. Button found at Crown Point State Historic Site, New York. Photo: courtesy of René Chartrand.

Source 5 – a '15' button c. 1759 (Fig. 5)

The Regimental Headquarters of the Prince of Wales's Own Regiment of Yorkshire possesses a '15' button which is believed to have been recovered from the Heights of Abraham, the scene of General Wolfe's epic assault against the French at Quebec in 1759. It bears a design of *J5*. In the 18th century, '1' was often written as a 'J'. The button is similar to that shown in Parkyn (1956: 118).

Historical background to buttons found on *Invincible*

Why were there so many different regimental numbered buttons found on the wreck-site from regiments that were not serving in North America?

Figure 5. 15th Regiment of Foot button recovered from the Heights of Abraham, diameter 24mm. Photo courtesy of J. M. Cubiss.

Between November 1757 and April 1758 requests were made from Barrington, the Secretary of War, to Cleveland, the Secretary to the Admiralty, for individual officers of the 6th, 13th, 14th, and 57th to take passage to Gibraltar (PRO, 1758a). Although *Invincible* was destined for Halifax in Canada, the voyage at that time of year would be southwards, with possible calls at Vigo and the Canaries where these officers could disembark. They would then make their way to Gibraltar; such arrangements were regularly authorised. Passages for officers going to North America, India and Jamaica were also requested which, along with the others, may explain the number of different regimental buttons found.

Another letter (PRO, 1758a) from Barrington to Admiral Boscawen dated 13 February 1758, informs Boscawen that two companies of the second battalion of the 34th and 37th, and 15 unattached officers were to go onboard the Fleet, as reinforcements. A further letter of March 1758 (PRO, 1758b) states that the mattresses of the 34th and 37th were to be removed from the wreck of the *Invincible*. This confirms the presence of the troops on board *Invincible*, and the 15 unattached officers may have been the 15 supernumeries on her muster list. Were they the staff of General Amherst, the newly appointed Commander-in-Chief of North America, who was to have taken passage but was late arriving from Germany? He later sailed on 16 March in the *Dublin*, which replaced *Invincible* following her stranding.

Another entry in *Invincible*'s log for 10 February 1758 reads:

'Rec'd from the Royall Arms 2 Liet's: a Sarg': and Corpes 42 soldiers part of Corn': Wallises Regiment' (PRO 1758c)

Cornwallis's Regiment was the 24th and a single 24th button (Button 5) was among those recovered.

Other buttons

A gold seal (Fig. 6) bearing the crest of the Howe Family has been found. Brigadier General George Augustus, 3rd Viscount Howe, was already in North America and this could have been amongst further baggage in transit; or perhaps, in the baggage of his younger brother, Lieutenant-Colonel William, 5th Viscount Howe, commanding Officer of Anstruther's 58th Regiment, who was on his way to North America. The Howe connection may explain the finding of the 'H' button (Appendix B Annex A, Button 14). The Howe brothers were 'dandies' in their day, and wearing their own 'H' buttons would have been in character.

Two of the buttons found were for the '8th Armagh' and 'RWM' (Fig. 2, nos 24 and 26). What were their origins? In 1756, Prime Minister Pitt ordered 'Militia' and 'volunteer' regiments to be raised. It is known that militia officers often volunteered to serve with line regiments on the outbreak of war as 'reinforcement officers'. The 'RWM' button is thought to stand for Royal Westminster Militia.

Figure 6. The Howe family crest – 13 x 15 mm. Photo: Tony Cullen.

Fouled anchor buttons

Fouled anchor buttons were worn by maritime regiment and marine officers. One of those found was silver but the majority were pewter with a thin layer of copper, a copper wash, that gave a gold appearance. One cast fouled anchor button still had the yellow twine wrapped around the boss of the button.

Another anchor button is different (Appendix B Annex A, button 22). It is dome-shaped, made of thin brass embossed with the fouled anchor and traces of gilding; the back is missing, but there are traces of glue where the back would have been fixed. This type was known during the early and mid-18th century as a composite 'shell button' and is further proof that the anchor emblem was worn in 1758. This button may have belonged to a naval officer rather than a marine. Thus predating the official introduction of the fouled anchor on naval officers' uniforms in 1774.

Button trademarks pre-1758

Some *Invincible* buttons were marked on the back with the names and addresses of the makers – 'I. Nutting Covent Garden', 'I. McGowan Kings Square Soho London', and a single button with the initials 'ISI'. At this period 'I' and 'J' were interchangeable and 'I Nutting' almost certainly refers to Joseph Nutting – for family details see Appendix B Annex A. Experts question makers' names on buttons in the 1750s, and hitherto it has been accepted that they were not introduced until the 1800s.

Trademarks were found on other artefacts such as pewter plates, spoons, shoe buckles and pursers' weights. Another wreck, the *Ramillies* (1760) has shoe buckles with various makers' names including 'I Turner', similar to an *Invincible* buckle – see Chapter 6 Figures 324 and 325. It would be fair to say that the practice was not uncommon in the mid-18th century; buttons would have been no exception.

Button styles

Of great interest are the style and construction of *Invincible*'s buttons. Most authorities say that in the first half of the 18th century, buttons were dome-shaped, with a bone or wooden back or former, and fastened with catgut (Barker 1977: 376; Houart 1977: 18; Parkyn 1956: 3–4; Squire 1972: 3).

Around 1760, they became flat with a long metal shank and were cast in pewter for rank and file, and silver or gold for officers. Buttons were generally small but became larger in the 1770s.

This belief is not supported by *Invincible*'s buttons. There is a whole range of types: domed with wooden and bone backs, one-piece semi-domed cast pewter, flat cast pewter, three-piece brass 'shell type', and large 29mm diameter brass flat buttons. Some of the cast buttons had the maker's name on the back. Many of the regimental buttons have a thin layer of copper covering the pewter, giving the appearance of 'gilding' and may well be officers' buttons. It seems that there was no transition period for domed, semi-domed to flat in the 1750s but that many styles were in use at the same time.

The recovery of many types of shoe similarly establishes beyond doubt that many different styles were being worn at the same time and dispels another clothing myth.

A 1758 War Office document

A War Office document (PRO 1758d) entitled: 'Facings Linings Buttons and Lace proposed by Rg Colonels of the New Regiments … with the Rank of the Regiment in the Center within a wreath of Roses and Thistles'. While the document is ambiguous as to whether: ' Rank of the Regiment in the Center …' refers to buttons, it does confirm that colonels were designing their own buttons and needed War Office approval. This particular document refers to the raising of Regiments 61 to 80. Certainly, numbered buttons were not the only part of military dress that were unofficial. It is known that in 1755 the 30th Grenadiers were wearing fur instead of the standard cloth mitre caps; their button with the Roman numeral XXX and crown, was one of the buttons recovered (Button 6). A 1765 Supplementary Royal Warrant directed the Grenadiers of the 14th Regiment to wear tall caps of black bearskin with their regimental number; a 14th button is also among those recovered (Button4).

Conclusions

Research shows that the mid-18th century was a transitional period in naval and military development, including dress. The clothing warrant of 1767 would have standardised dress for the whole Army, and made official some of the innovations sponsored by regimental colonels. Colonels vied with each other over the appearance of their respective regiments, and the introduction of numbered buttons was part of this development.

Closed archaeological contexts, notably wreck sites, provide an invaluable check on the interpretation of limited documentary evidence. The value of the *Invincible* site is that is constitutes a precisely dated time capsule. All buttons listed in Appendix B Annex A were in existence on that fateful Sunday morning in February 1758.

Acknowledgements

The authors wish to record their thanks to: Leslie Dury for his research into the Nutting family, Major H. G. R. Boscawen for his research into the Louisbourg Expedition; Brigadier J. M. Cubiss for information on the 15th button; René Chartrand of Parks Canada for information on the 50th and 51st buttons; and Charles Burke, Project Archaeologist, Fortress of Louisbourg for his briefing on the excavations and in particular for showing us the 65th button. Thanks are due to John Bethell for his dedicated work in clarifying the button photographs and to Jane Bingeman for her help in editing the report.

References

Anon. 1757, *A System of Camp Discipline*. London.

Barker, D. 1977, British Naval Officers Buttons 1748–1975. *MM*, 63: 373–387.

Bingeman, J. M. 1985, Interim report on artefacts recovered from *Invincible* (1758) between 1979 and 1984. *IJNA*, 14: 191–210.

Houart, V. 1977, *Buttons – a Collector's Guide*. London.

Parkman, F. 1899, *Montcalm and Wolfe*. Toronto.

Parkyn, H. G. 1956, *Shoulder-Belt Plates and Buttons*. Aldershot.

Public Records Office, 1758a, *War Office 'out' Letters*. WO 4/55.

Public Records Office, 1758b, *Secretary's 'out' Letters to Public Officers*. ADM 2/522, 13th February to 11th July.

Public Records Office, 1758c, ADM 51/471.

Public Records Office, 1758d, WO 7/26.

Squire, G. 1972, *Buttons – A Guide for Collectors*. London.

Appendix B Annex A

1. 1st Footguards	Button in doomed cast pewter, shank missing. 21mm diameter. Interlaced 'GR' inside garter with *Honi Soit Qui Mal Y Pense* and a Queen's crown above. Backmark: *I. Nutting and Son, Covent Garden*. Possibly from baggage of Captain William Amherst, 1st Footguards and ADC to General Jeffrey Amherst. In an order of 1771, the 1st Footguards were to wear flat gilt buttons; previous buttons were domed. The Footguards of the Hanoverian Regiments had the Royal Coat of Arms on their buttons. (Inv/80/183).
2. 6th Regiment of Foot	Flat cast pewter button, 23mm diameter, with rope rim and French circle design with dot, and bird cage fastening. Guise's officers requesting passage to Gibraltar. (Inv/81/066).
3. 13th Regiment of Foot	Flat cast pewter button, 16mm diameter, with *13* within an eight-point star. Iron shanks missing on all three buttons, their reverse inscribed 'I. Nutting & Son, Covent Garden'. Pulteney's Officers requesting passage to Gibraltar. (Inv/80/145, 147 and 227).
4. 14th Regiment of Foot	Flat cast pewter button, 24mm diameter, copper washed. French circle design with dot. Jefferye's Officers requesting passage to Gibraltar.
5. 24th Regiment of Foot	Flat cast pewter button, 17mm diameter, copper washed. The *24* within a continuous wreath circle. Cornwallis's Marines – a sergeant and 45 men were onboard. (No 'Inv' number – recovered by J. Broomhead pre-survey).
6. 30th Regiment of foot	Flat cast pewter button, 16.5mm diameter, iron shank missing. Motif: XXX with Queen's crown above. Loudoun's reinforcement officers. Two buttons. (No 'Inv' number – recovered by J. Broomhead pre-survey; Inv/81/147).
7. 39th Regiment of Foot	Domed cast pewter button, 14.8mm diameter, floral wreaths design on the outer rim. Adlercron's Regiment from the Portsmouth Area embarking for East Indies, an additional company raised in 1755. (Inv/83/122).
8. 39th Regiment of Foot	Domed cast pewter button, 20.5mm diameter, floral wreath design as on the smaller 14.8mm diameter button. (Inv/87/84).
9. 43rd Regiment of Foot	Flat cast pewter button, 16mm diameter, copper washed. *43* inside a laurel wreath design. Iron shank missing. Backmark: *I. Nutting and Son, Covent Garden*. Kennedy's Regiment known to be in North America. (Inv/81/222).
10. 57th Regiment of Foot	Slightly domed cast pewter button, 16mm diameter, *57* with rope edge. Iron shank

missing. Cunningham's Regiment was serving at Gibraltar. Robin Readon, Ensign of the 57th, requested passage to Gibraltar on 9 February 1758. (Inv/81/162).

11. 59th Regiment of Foot	Flat cast pewter button, 23mm diameter, copper washed, shank missing. Queen's crown above *59*. Montague's Regiment was in Ireland; possibly an officer on secondment. (Inv/80/255, Inv/83/113, 114, 116 and 125)
12. 59th Regiment of Foot	Diameter 17mm Details as for 23mm diameter button. (Inv/83/126).
13. 64th Regiment of Foot	Semi-domed cast pewter button, 23mm diameter, copper washed. Iron shank missing. At the beginning of the Seven Years War the 11th Regiment of Foot raised a second battalion which was formed into a separate company designated the 64th Regiment of Foot. (Inv/80/251).
14. 'H' button	Flat cast pewter button, 16mm diameter. Possible 'Howe' family connection. Backmark: *I. McGowan, King Sq., Soho, London*. (Inv/88/83).
15. 'ISI' button	Semi-domed cast pewter button, 20mm diameter, plain face. Backmark: *ISI*. Unfortunately crushed when trapped between timbers in the wreck. (Inv/84/202).
16. Fouled Anchor	Flat cast pewter button, 17mm diameter, iron shank missing. Fouled anchor with rope edge. Backmark: *I. Nutting and Son, Covent Garden* (reading round the outside, not reversed). (Inv/83/182).
17. Fouled Anchor	Flat cast pewter button, 17mm diameter. Fouled anchor with plain edge. Backmark: *I. Nutting and Son, Covent Garden*. (Inv/83/124).
18. Fouled Anchor	Semi-domed cast pewter button, copper washed, 17mm diameter. Fouled anchor with rope edge. The anchor stock is smaller and at a more pronounced angle. (Inv/85/6 and 7, Inv/87/40).
19. Fouled anchor	Large fouled anchor button, 23mm diameter, rope-rimmed and copper washed. (In/85/005, Inv/NK).
20. Fouled Anchor	Semi-domed cast pewter button, 18mm diameter. Stock of fouled anchor at a pronounced angle. (Inv/80/252).
21. Fouled Anchor	Semi-domed cast pewter button, 18mm diameter. Fouled anchor with rope edge. Worn and scratched face. (Inv/87/209).
22. Fouled Anchor	Brass composite shell type button, 25mm diameter, with fouled anchor and traces of gilding. Wooden back missing. Typical button construction of the period. (No 'Inv' number – recovered by J. Broomhead 18 July 1979 pre-survey).
23. Union Jack Pattern	Button made of leather, 21mm diameter. Two examples. (Inv/83/91, Inv/84/322).
24. 8th Armagh	Semi-domed cast pewter button, 15.5mm diameter. An *8* in a circle surmounted by a Queen's Crown and the word *Armagh* underneath. Possibly a reinforcement officer or volunteer for line service with a regiment. The 8th Armagh Militia was previously thought to have been raised in 1760. (Inv/84/280).
25. Tudor Rose Motif	Brass composite shell-type button, 16mm diameter. Tudor rose motif, wooden back missing. Worn by naval lieutenants from early to mid 18th century. (Inv/84/157).
26. RWM button	Flat cast pewter button, 16mm diameter. Eastern crown above shields depicting, on the left a portcullis and on the right three sabres; below *RWM*, thought to stand for 'Royal Westminster Militia', a most unusual design. Militia officers are known to have volunteered during the Napoleonic Wars for service in line regiments; perhaps this happened in earlier wars. (Inv/80/182).
27. Death Head button	Flat button with silk twine woven around bone former, known as a death head button, 22mm diameter. Fawn coloured, in good condition. Similarly styled black buttons were worn by 19th-century naval chaplains. (Inv/87/199).

Appendix B Annex B

Nutting family tree

Joseph (1)	Nutting (1660–1722) engraver. Married Ellen and had six children all born at Sandon, Hertfordshire. Their eldest son was:
Joseph (2)	Nutting (1702–?) Occupation unknown. Married Ann Shelton in 1733 and had two children. The eldest was named John (1734) and the youngest was:
Joseph (3)	Nutting (1736–?) Button maker. Married Elizabeth in 1778 and their two children were both born in King Street, Covent Garden. Their eldest being:
John George	Nutting (1779–1864) Apprentice button maker on 2 October 1793 and gained his freedom (i.e. qualified) on 6 January 1801. He registered his mark (*I. Nutting and Son*) with his father, Joseph (3), on 18 March 1803. Married Grace Henderson in 1804.

Supposition

Since Joseph (1) was an engraver and Joseph (3) was known to be a button maker, it is not inconceivable that Joseph (2) could also have been in the button business as the two trades are very akin to each other. There is a gap in documentary evidence but it seems likely that the father and son (Josephs (2) and (3)), could have been in partnership making buttons in the mid-1750s and the source of the military buttons found in *Invincible*.

Trademarks

The trademarks: *I. Nutting and son, King Street, Covent Garden*, and *I. Nutting and Son, Covent Garden*. would seem appropriate. The latter was easier to use as the former was cramped on the back of a 17mm button and was found only on one fouled anchor button (Inv/83/124) with a plain edge; this appears to be an early attempt at making an 'anchor' button. The use of 'I' and 'J' were synonymous in writing of this period, and discounts any confusion over the initials.

Trade Directories

A question often posed is why the Nutting button business in King Street, Covent Garden was not mentioned in Trade Directories before 1784/5. These directories were quite small in the mid-1750s and covered a relatively small number of firms. It seems reasonable to suppose that as the directories expanded, the Nutting family firm should have an entry from 1784, when they were better established.

Small Fouled anchor button No. 17 (Inv/83/124) Manufactured by I. Nutting and Son.

Lead	(Pb)	35.627%
Tin	(Sn)	56.616%
Iron	(Fe)	1.120%
Copper	(Cu)	6.635%

Large Fouled anchor button No. 19 (Inv/85/005) manufacturer not known.

Lead	(Pb)	60.041%
Tin	(Sn)	1.823%
Iron	(Fe)	17.235%
Copper	(Cu)	20.900%

Index

Page numbers in *italic* show illustrations.